W9-ARX-114

THE FIRST-TIME MANAGER

Fourth Edition

THE
FIRST-TIME
MANAGER

Fourth Edition

Loren B. Belker

American Management Association

New York • Atlanta • Boston • Chicago • Kansas City • San Francisco • Washington, D.C.
Brussels • Mexico City • Tokyo • Toronto

This book is available at a special
discount when ordered in bulk quantities.
For information, contact Special Sales Department,
AMACOM, a division of American Management Association,
1601 Broadway, New York, NY 10019.

This publication is designed to provide accurate and authoritative information in regard to the subject matter covered. It is sold with the understanding that the publisher is not engaged in rendering legal, accounting, or other professional service. If legal advice or other expert assistance is required, the services of a competent professional person should be sought.

Library of Congress Cataloging-in-Publication Data

Belker, Loren B.
   The first-time manager / Loren B. Belker. — 4th ed.
      p.   cm.
   Includes index.
   ISBN 0-8144-7940-5
   1. Supervision of employees.   2. Office management.   I. Title.
HF5549.B355   1997
   658.3'02—dc20   96-39055
                                                            CIP

© 1997 AMACOM, a division of
American Management Association, New York.
All rights reserved.
Printed in the United States of America.

This publication may not be reproduced,
stored in a retrieval system,
or transmitted in whole or in part,
in any form or by any means, electronic,
mechanical, photocopying, recording, or otherwise,
without the prior written permission of AMACOM,
a division of American Management Association,
1601 Broadway, New York, NY 10019.

Printing number

10   9   8   7   6   5   4   3   2   1

For **Jeff** and **Maggie**, with appreciation for all the joy you have brought to our lives.

Contents

Acknowledgments

People often have a greater impact on our lives than they're aware of at the time.

I would like to acknowledge my good friend Professor Bill Torrence from the Department of Management at the University of Nebraska, who read an early draft of the first edition of this book and offered encouragement at a critical time in the writing of the original manuscript. His straightforward advice was crucial.

The many people who have been in my management seminars have done as much, or more, for me than I have for them. Their desire to improve their management skills has been their first step in becoming humane and enlightened leaders of people. They've been willing to set aside previously held attitudes of what a manager ought to be.

My sincere thanks to my editor and friend Adrienne Hickey, Senior Acquisitions and Planning Editor at AMACOM. Her insights and encouragement on the revisions and new editions have played a major role in the success of this book.

Finally, my undying gratitude to my wife, best friend, and life's companion, Darlene. Her courage has been an inspiration to all who know her.

Introduction

So you're going to manage people. Your life will never be the same.

You're embarking on a stage of your career that will be an unending challenge. That challenge will be the achievement of goals or objectives through others. That is what supervision and management are all about.

Application of the principles described here should benefit anyone who is about to embark on a managerial career. Our relationship with other human beings is the most challenging opportunity that exists for us. It covers all aspects of our lives.

There are many books on the subject of management, but few of them address themselves to—or zero in on—those individuals who are about to begin a career of leading others. These people are not interested in a lot of academic claptrap; rather, they are in a state of mixed emotion—absolutely delighted with the promotion and absolutely panic-stricken with the realization that from now on they'll be judged by how well their subordinates perform.

This book is for those people, not for top management with thirty years' experience, even though many top managers would do well to refresh their acquaintance with some of the basic principles that will be discussed.

Since the first edition of this book appeared, I've conducted numerous seminars for first-time managers, and some for experienced managers. One comment made repeatedly by participants is, "My boss needs this information even more than I do." This then, creates for the new manager the problem of how you manage in an environment where your own manager violates principles and concepts that you practice and believe in. This new edition provides some insight and assistance in that arena.

Many experienced managers have moved away from the basics. While they understand the principles, their management style is contradictory. The late football coach Vince Lombardi got back to basics by holding a football in his hands and declaring to his players, "Gentlemen, this is a football." Perhaps when it comes to management, we could paraphrase it and say, "Executives, this is a human being."

I've attempted to write this guide in a conversational manner, as if I were talking directly to you. I trust you'll find it easy to refer back to specific areas when problems arise in the future. After a few months of managing people, reread the book. Some of the concepts may take on additional usefulness at that time.

Several new chapters have been added in this fourth edition, and many chapters have been modified or enlarged. You will note the significance of the attitudes you bring to management, and how most of the problems you encounter are not technical in nature: the role appreciation plays; the way things are, and the way some think they are; management style; coaching; the broad base of experiences an effective manager needs to bring to the daily environment; and other tools for your management toolbox.

Lastly, almost all of the problems you will encounter as a new manager may be new to you, but they've been experienced by many others. The problems you encounter are balanced by the joy and satisfaction of a management job well done.

Thanks for deciding to spend some time with me.

One

The New Kid on the Block

1

How People Are Chosen as Supervisors

Unfortunately, many companies don't go through a very thorough process in choosing those who are to be moved into managerial positions. Often the judgment is based solely on how well the person is performing in the currently assigned task. The best performer doesn't always make the best manager, although many companies still make the choice on that basis. The theory is that successful past performance is the best indicator of future success.

It's important that you have a record of being successful, but being the best operator doesn't make you the best leader, for a number of reasons. If the current job doesn't require that you work cooperatively with others, you could be performing well as a loner.

So the fact that you're a good performer, even though it demonstrates a success pattern, doesn't necessarily mean you'll be successful as a manager. Being a manager requires skills beyond those of being a satisfactory operator.

Management Isn't for Everyone

Some companies have management training programs. They vary from excellent to horrible. Too often the program is given to people who have already been in managerial positions for a number of years. Even experienced managers should be periodically given refresher courses in management style and techniques. If a training program has any merit, it should be given to individuals who are being considered for management positions. This helps them avoid mistakes, and also gives the trainees the opportunity to see whether they will be comfortable leading others.

Unfortunately, too many organizations are still using the "swim or sink" method of management training. All who move into supervisory positions have to figure it out on their own. This method assumes that everyone intuitively knows how to manage. They don't. Managing people is crucial to the success of any organization, and in too many cases, it is left to chance. Anyone who has worked for any length of time has observed situations where promotions didn't work out and the person asked for the old job back. There's an old cliché that goes like this: "Don't wish too hard for something, because you might get it." In too many companies the opportunities for promotion are limited if you don't go into management. As a result some people go into management who shouldn't be there, and wouldn't want to be if other chances for salary increases and promotion existed.

I conducted a series of management seminars for a company that used an enlightened approach to this problem of moving the wrong people into management. Everyone likely to be considered for a first-line management position was invited to attend an all-day seminar on what is involved in the management of people. Included were some simple but typical management problems. When they were invited to attend, they were told by the company, "If after attending this seminar you decide that the management of people is not something you want to do, just say so. That decision will in no way affect other nonmanagement promotion possibilities nor future salary decisions in your current position." Around 500 people attended these seminars, and approximately 20 percent decided they did not want to move into management. After getting a brief taste of it, approximately 100 people knew they would not make good managers, but they were still valuable employees. Too many people accept a management promotion because they feel (often rightly so) that they will be dead-ended if they reject the promotion.

The Octopus

There are those who really believe that if you want something done right, you'd better do it yourself. People with this attitude rarely make good leaders because they have difficulty delegating responsibility. We've all seen them: They delegate only those trivial tasks that any idiot could perform, and anything meaningful they keep themselves. As a result, they work evenings and weekends and take a briefcase home as well. I'm not putting down overtime, because all of us occasionally must devote some extra time to the job, but people who follow this pattern as a way of life are poor managers. They have so little faith in their subordinates that they trust them with nothing important. What they're really saying is that they don't know how to properly train their people.

There's usually a turnover problem in a section with this kind of manager. The employees are usually more qualified than the "octopus" believes (the term *octopus* is used because such a leader reaches out and takes personal possession of all the responsible tasks), and they soon tire of handling only trivia.

I suspect you know of an octopus in your own office. I hope you're not working for one, because you'll have a difficult time being promoted. Caught up in your impossible situation, you're not given anything responsible to do, and as a result you never get a chance to demonstrate what you can do. You seldom get a recommendation for promotion from Mr. Octopus—assuming for a moment that he's a man. He's convinced that the reason he has to do all the work is his people don't accept responsibility. He can never admit that it's because he refuses to delegate.

Mr. Octopus is a tragedy and should never have been placed in a managerial position. When he is passed over for promotion, he becomes quite bitter because no one works harder than he does. Obviously, his efforts are not much appreciated. He set out to make himself indispensable, and in so doing, he made himself unpromotable. Another reason he is a tragic figure is that the person could be an effective employee in the hands of a skilled manager. He simply is in the wrong job, and frankly that is a promotion error. If promotions into the managerial positions are made too casually, there will be a long time to live with the unfortunate consequences.

Particular attention has been given to Mr. Octopus, primarily so that you won't allow yourself to fall into this trap. If you do become this kind of monster, it probably follows on your having just received your last promotion up the corporate ladder—unless the top executive is an octopus himself. In that case the whole organization is in trouble, and there's a good chance the top executive will die a premature death. This is not to imply that every executive who dies prematurely is an octopus manager.

One other unvarying trait of Mr. Octopus is that he seldom takes his vacation all at once. He takes it a couple of days at a time because the company can't function longer than that without him. Before going on his vacation, he'll leave specific instructions as to what work is to be saved until his return. In some situations, he'll leave a phone number where he can be reached in an emergency. Of course, he defines what the emergency might be. He even says to his wife, "I can't even get away from the problems for a few days without being bothered." What he doesn't say is that this is exactly the way he wants it because it makes him feel so important. I've known octopus managers whose retirement years were demolished because retirement meant abolition of their reason for living, their dedication to the job, and their preceived indispensability.

The Chosen Few

In many organizations, new managers are chosen because of the current supervisor's recommendation. If you're fortunate, you're working for such a person. This type of leader gives subordinates a great deal of latitude; as a result, the department achieves a reputation as a breeding ground for future managerial talent. (We'll talk more in Chapter 25 about how you can develop into this kind of manager.)

People are also chosen to head a function because they're related to the boss. Consider yourself fortunate if you're not in such a company. Even if you *are* related to the boss, it's very difficult to assume additional responsibility under such circumstances. You doubtless have the authority, but today's businesses aren't dictatorships and people won't perform well for you just because you've been anointed from on high. So, if you're the boss's son or daughter, you really have to prove yourself. You'll get surface respect, but let's face it—it's what people really think of you, not what they say to you, that matters and that affects how they perform. If you're related to the boss, you might consider getting your experience elsewhere before taking on a supervisory position in your relative's firm. Since the vast majority of you are not in that position, let's see what other problems you face.

In most organizations, you're not chosen for a managerial position because of your technical knowledge. You're chosen because someone has seen the spark of leadership in you. That's the spark you must start developing. Leadership is difficult to define. A leader is a person others look to for direction, a person whose judgment is respected because it's usually sound. As you exercise your judgment and develop the capacity to make sound decisions, it becomes a self-perpetuating characteristic. Your faith in your own decision-making power is fortified. That feeds your self-confidence, and with more self-confidence you become less reluctant to make difficult decisions.

Some of the country's larger corporations do have formal management programs. Often they recruit people directly out of college. As a result, many people already in the corporation who would make great managers if given the opportunity are frozen out. Many of these programs are well constructed and broad based. People chosen off the college campus may or may not make outstanding managers of people. Just as it is a mistake to assume that a good personal producer will always make a satisfactory manager of people, so it may be a mistake to assume that someone placed in a management program will be a good manager. The advantage of such programs may be that trainees are not put into positions of supervising people until they've gone through the training. Such programs are most successful when they select people from many sources, including sources within the organization.

A leader is a person who can see into the future and visualize the result of his or her decision making. A leader is also a person who can set aside matters of personality and make decisions based on fact. This doesn't mean you ignore the human element—you never ignore it, but you deal always with the facts themselves, not with people's emotional perception of those facts.

People are chosen to be managers for a wide variety of reasons. If you're chosen for sound reasons, your acceptance by your new subordinates will, for the most part, be much easier to come by.

2

The First Few Months

Your first week on the job as a manager will be unusual, to say the least. If you're a student of human behavior, you'll observe some surprising developments.

Settling In

Don't believe that everyone is happy about the choice of the new kid on the block. Some of your co-workers will feel *they* should have been chosen. They may be jealous of your new promotion and secretly hope you fall on your face.

Others, the office "yes people," will immediately start playing up to you. As the chosen one, you can be their ticket to success. Their objective isn't all bad, but their method of operation leaves something to be desired.

Others will put you to the test early. They may ask you questions to see if you know the answers. If you don't, they'll want to see if you'll admit it or if you'll try to bluff your way through it. Some may ask you questions you can't possibly know the answers to yet, for the sheer delight of embarrassing you.

Most—you hope the majority—will adopt a wait-and-see attitude. They're not going to condemn or praise you until they see how you perform. This attitude is healthy and all you really have a right to expect.

You'll be measured initially against your predecessor in the position. If that other's performance was miserable, yours will look great by comparison even if it's mediocre. If you follow a highly capable performer, your adjustment will be tougher. Before you begin thinking it's best to follow a miserable performer, consider the load of tough problems you're inheriting from your inept predecessor; that's why you're there. The highly capable predecessor is probably gone because he or she was promoted. So, in either case, you have a big job ahead of you.

One of your first decisions should be to refrain from immediately instituting changes in the method of operation. (In abnormal situations, top management may have instructed you to go in and make certain immediate changes because of the seriousness of the situation. However, in such cases it is usually announced that changes will be forthcoming.) Above all, be patient. If you make changes immediately, you'll be resented. Your actions will be construed as arrogance and an insult to your predecessor. Many young new leaders make their own lives more difficult by assuming they have to use all their newfound power immediately. The key word should rather be *restraint*. Whether or not you want to admit it, you're the one who's on trial with your subordinates, not they with you.

This is a good time to make an important point about your own attitude. Many young managers communicate rather well upward to their superiors, but poorly downward to their subordinates. Your subordinates will have more to say about your future than your superiors. You're going to be judged by how well your section or department functions, so the people who now work for you are the most important in your business life. Believe it or not, they're more important even than the president of your company. This bit of knowledge has always seemed obvious to me, yet many new managers spend almost all their time planning their upward communication and give only a passing glance to the people who really control their future.

You undoubtedly know members of the management team who come strolling into the office well after the beginning hour. This is a luxury you can't afford. It's unreasonable to expect subordinates to consider it important to be punctual and start work at the designated time if it's not important to you. Leading by example is still a good concept. This is an area where I recommend that you deviate from your predecessor's practice immediately. Your people will respect you because you observe the same rules that they're expected to observe. The boss who comes in late loses more than the productivity for that hour. That's indeed the smallest part of the lost cost. How do you measure the cost of the halfhearted work that takes place before the top executive comes into the office? It's not that the staff won't work unless they're being watched; rather, they reflect their own manager's attitude. You can't blame them for responding in that manner.

Storehouse of Authority

If there is one area that many new managers blunder into, it is the use of authority. This is particularly true of those who are navigating their way through a self-directed "swim or sink" method of on-the-job training. It is the idea that because you now have the authority of management, you must start using it, and you must use and display it in a big way. It may be the biggest mistake that new managers make.

View the authority of the new position as you would a storehouse of supplies. The fewer times you take supplies from the storehouse, the greater is the supply that remains there for when it is *really* needed.

The newly appointed manager who starts acting like "the boss" and begins issuing orders and other directives is off to a bad start. While you may not hear the remarks directly, the typical comments made behind the back of such a misguided manager might be, "Boy, is she drunk with power," or "This job has really gone to his head," or "His hat size has gone up two sizes since he was promoted." You don't need this kind of problem.

If you don't go to the storehouse of authority too often, the authority you may have to use in an emergency is more effective because it is so infrequently displayed.

The people you supervise know that you are the manager.

They know that the request you make carries the authority of the position. The vast majority of the time, it's unnecessary to use that authority.

There's a term in the creative arts called *understatement*. For the most part, it means that what is left unsaid may be as important as what is said. This is true with the use of authority. A direction given as a request is a managerial type of under-statement. If the response is not forthcoming, you can always clarify or add a bit of authority. On the other hand, if you use all your authority to achieve a task, and then discover by the reaction that you've used too much, the damage is done. It's difficult, if not impossible, to de-escalate the overuse of that authority.

In short, don't assume that you need to use the authority of your position. Perhaps the greatest by-product of this softer approach is you are not building a negative image that may be nearly impossible to erase later.

The Personal Touch

Sometime during the first sixty days on the job you should plan on having a personal conversation with each of the people in your area of responsibility. Don't do this the first week or so. Give your subordinates a chance to get used to the idea that you're there. When it comes, the conversation should be formal in nature. Ask your subordinates into your office for an unhurried discussion about anything that's on their mind. Do no more talking yourself than necessary. This first formal discussion is not designed for you to communicate with the others; it's designed to open lines of communication from them to you. (Have you ever noticed that the more you allow the other person to talk, the higher you'll be rated as a brilliant conversationalist?)

Although the employee's personal concerns are important, it's preferable to restrict the discussion to work-related topics. Sometimes it's difficult to define these limits because problems at home may be troubling the employee more than anything else, but at all times you must avoid getting into a situation where you're giving personal advice. Just because you've been anointed as the boss, that doesn't make you an expert on all the personal problems confronting your people. Listen to them; often that's what they need more than anything else—someone to listen to them.

Some people will overstay these visits. More about methods of controlling the length of these conversations will be discussed in Chapter 4, "Learning to Listen."

Getting to Know Them

Now let's get back to your conversation with your subordinates. The purpose is to give them the opportunity to open communications with you. Show a genuine interest in their concerns; learn what their ambitions are with the company. Ask questions that will get them to expand on their point of view. You can't fake genuine interest in others; you're doing this because you care about the employee's well-being. Such attention is advantageous to both of you. If you can help employees achieve their goals, they'll be more productive; what's more important, they'll feel they're making progress toward their goals.

You'll note that I don't talk about happy employees because, frankly, I don't know if it's good for a company to have happy employees. Many people think *happy* means satisfied, and a satisfied employee is one who is content. An employee who is content is unlikely to reach out for something better and thus is probably not as productive as she could be.

So your goal in these early conversations is to let your subordinates know you care about them as individuals and you're there to help them achieve their goals. Let them know you want to help them solve whatever problems they may be having with the job. Establish a comfort zone in which they can deal with you. Make them feel that it's perfectly natural for them to discuss small problems with you. By discussing small problems and small irritants, you can probably avoid most of the larger problems.

You'll discover in your first few months as a manager that your technical abilities are not nearly as important as your human abilities. The majority of your problems are going to revolve around the human and not the technical aspects of the job. Unless your responsibilities are technically complex, you'll find that if you have outstanding human skills, you can overlook your minor technical deficiencies. Conversely, even if you're the most technically competent manager in the office, without human skills you'll have great difficulty.

Friends in the Department

One of the problems many new executives confront is handling friendships with people in the department who now become their subordinates. This is a difficult situation and I'm sure there's no perfect answer.

It's obvious that you shouldn't have to give up your friendships simply because you've received a promotion. However, you don't want your friendships to hurt your performance or the performance of your friends.

You can't allow your friendships to interfere with your method of operation. A subordinate who's really a friend will understand the dilemma you find yourself in. It is precisely this dilemma that causes some executives to believe that promoted managers should be brought in from other areas. It minimizes the chances that they'll know their subordinates too well and have close friends within the department.

You must be certain that co-workers who were your friends before you became their supervisor receive the same treatment as everyone else. They must not be treated worse merely to prove to the others how unbiased you are.

If you've usually taken your coffee breaks with certain people in your department, you should consider adopting a rotation policy so that within a short period you'll have had your coffee break with all your subordinates. This practice seems preferable to discontinuing the sessions and going with fellow supervisors. That would be construed as your moving up the corporate ladder: "Her old friends aren't good enough for her anymore."

There is a temptation to use your old friend in the department as a confidant. You do not want to give the impression that you are playing favorites. In fact, you must not play favorites. Never discuss the performance or your concerns about one employee with another. First, this is a double-edged sword. The chances that the discussion will be held confidential is virtually nonexistent. Second, eventually the person you confide in will have this thought: "I wonder what he says about me to others when I'm not around." Using an employee in the department, even a friend, as a confidant will sow distrust and damage the confidence people need to have in you as manager. If you do need a confidant, it's preferable to use a supervisor in another department or section of the organization.

3

Building Confidence

Building confidence is a gradual process. One of your main goals is to develop the confidence of your employees, both in their own abilities and in their opinion of you. They must have confidence that you're competent at your job and that you're fair.

The Success Habit

Building confidence in employees is not an easy task. Do you believe success is habit forming? Failure can also become a habit. Confidence is built on success, so give your people horses they can ride. Especially in dealing with new employees, assign them tasks they can master. Build in them the habit of being successful, starting small with small successes.

Occasionally a subordinate will perform a task incorrectly or just plain blow it. How you handle such situations has a great impact on the confidence of employees. Never correct them in front of others. "Praise in public, criticize in private," the old credo goes—it still has a lot of management truth in it.

Even when you talk to a subordinate in private about an error, your function is to train that person to recognize the nature of the problem so as not to make the same error again. Your attitude about errors will speak louder to an employee than the words you use. Your statements must be directed toward correcting the misunderstanding that led to the error and not toward personal judgment. Never say or do anything that will make the employee feel inadequate. You want to build confidence, not destroy it. If you get pleasure from making subordinates feel foolish, then you'd better start examining your own motives, because you can't build yourself up by tearing someone else down. Examine the error on the basis of what went wrong, where the misunderstanding occurred, and go on from there. Treat the small error routinely; don't make it bigger than it really is.

Let's briefly discuss the "praise in public" part of the old credo. I used to believe in that concept until I found that it too sometimes created problems. The individual on the receiving end of the praise felt warm and fuzzy about the compliment, but others who were not so commended reacted negatively. The disappointment was then directed at the employee who was praised. That's why it's important to be cautious about praising in public. "Good work" and "I appreciate the great job you did on this" are about as far as you can go without creating a problem for the person you're attempting to reward. Why make life tougher for that employee by creating jealousy or resentment in the people he must work with eight hours a day? If you really want to praise someone expansively for outstanding performance, do it in the privacy of your office. You'll get the pluses without the negatives of resentment and jealousy from co-workers.

You can also build confidence by involving your people in some of the decision-making processes. Without delegating any of your supervisory responsibilities to them, allow them to have some major input into matters that affect them. A new task about to be performed in your area presents the opportunity to give your subordinates some input. Solicit ideas from them on how the new task might best be worked into the daily routine. Given this kind of participation, the new routine will succeed because it's everyone's routine, not just yours. This doesn't mean your staff is making decisions for you; what I'm suggesting is that by involving your people in the process that leads up to your decision, you'll have them working with you rather than accepting new systems imposed on them.

The Evils of Perfectionism

Some managers expect perfection from their employees. They know they won't get it but they feel they'll get closer to it by demanding it. Unfortunately, some executives really believe they can get perfection from employees. By insisting on perfection you may in fact defeat your own purposes: Some employees will become so self-conscious about making a mistake that they slow their performance down to a crawl to make absolutely certain they don't screw up. As a result, production goes way down. The company might be better off having a production of one hundred with five errors than a production of twenty with one error.

Another drawback to being a perfectionist is that everyone resents you for it. Your subordinates believe you're impossible to please and you prove it to them every day. You know what the acceptable standards for work performance are in your company; no one can blame you for wanting to be better than the average; but you'll have far more success if you get the employees involved in helping decide how to improve performance. If it's their plan, you have a significantly better chance of achieving your goal.

You can also build confidence by developing esprit de corps within your own area. Make sure, however, that the feeling you build is supportive of the prevailing company spirit and not in competition with it.

Decision Making

Some people agonize over every decision they have to make. If making decisions is a constant irritation for you, you should seriously question whether you ought to be in management. If you're already in management, perhaps what follows will lessen your fears and relieve your concerns.

I see two basic reasons why some people have trouble making decisions. First, they're not certain they have all the information necessary to make a decision; second, they're afraid of making a mistake and dreading the consequences.

It's unlikely that you'll ever be able to gather 100 percent of the information that might apply to a business situation. There's a shorthand for this process that you might call to mind when struggling with a decision: the 80/20 rule. In most management decisions, 80 percent of the information needed to make a decision becomes apparent in a relatively short period of time. The other 20 percent is much more difficult to secure. The search for that last 20 percent is not likely to change the decision you'll make. Many times, the new manager uses the search for the other 20 percent as rationalization to delay a decision.

Obviously, there's no way to know when you have exactly 80 percent of the information needed. The 80/20 rule merely means that the vast majority of the information needed comes much more quickly than the rest of it. The major point is that the delay in searching for the last 20 percent is not likely to change the decision you make.

A baseball player who bats .300 is called a millionaire. A business person batting .300 is called bankrupt. Most of the decisions you make are management and people decisions, and common sense plays a major role in the process. By application of these principles and common sense, you'll bat .980 or better.

There are, of course, occupations where the 80/20 rule should not apply. You don't want the pilot flying your jet plane using the 80/20 concept, nor do you want a brain surgeon following the rule. We are discussing management decisions and judgments where it is appropriate.

You will, of course, occasionally make a wrong decision. You're human. Let's close this section with a statement that may sum it up: You can get into more management difficulty by repeatedly refusing to make decisions, or by delaying unreasonably, than you can by occasionally making an incorrect decision.

4

Learning to Listen

One of the best-kept secrets of successful management is the ability to listen. Most new managers become very concerned about their ability to communicate. Too many managers have the mistaken idea that the minute they are promoted everyone is going to hang on to every word they say. They set out to fill that need. That is exactly the wrong approach. Such managers should remember they have two ears and one mouth; therefore, they ought to do twice as much listening as talking.

Listening is one of the most valuable traits that a new manager can demonstrate, for two important reasons: First, if you do a great deal of listening, you will not be thought of as a know-it-all, which is how most people perceive someone who talks too much. Second, by doing a lot of listening and little talking, you'll learn what is going on. You'll learn none of it by talking.

Most people are not good listeners, and we ought to examine why this is so.

The Poor Listener

Many people believe that the most beautiful sound in the world is their own voice. It's truly music to their ears. They can't get enough of it, so they require others to listen to it. Typically, such people are more interested in what they are going to say themselves than in what others are saying. Indeed, most people can remember nearly everything they've said and hardly any of what the other person has said. People listen partially. They are too busy thinking of the clever thing they are going to utter, "as soon as this idiot takes a breath and I can break in."

If you don't remember anything else about this chapter, you'll do yourself immeasurable good by recalling this statement: If you want to be thought of as a brilliant conversationalist, be a good listener.

Too many managers, both new and not so new, do too much talking and not enough listening. You learn very little while you are talking, but you can learn a great deal while listening. The new manager thinks that now that he's in charge, everyone is hanging on to every word. It's not by choice. We can't take any satisfaction in the fact that people reporting to us feel they have to listen. Ask yourself if they'd listen to your insight into the world's problems if they had a choice. They have no choice, since you're the boss. Don't take advantage. The more you talk, the more you run the risk of boring others. The more you listen, the more you learn. It seems like an obvious choice, especially for a manager of people.

Another reason people are not good listeners is the comprehension gap. Most people communicate at between 80 and 120 words per minute. Let's assume 100 words per minute as the average speaking speed. People can comprehend at a much higher rate. Those who have taken a rapid reading course, and who maintain the skill, can comprehend well over 1,000 words per minute. If someone is speaking at 100 words per minute to a listener who can comprehend at 1,000 words per minute, there is a 900-word-per-minute comprehension gap. A speaking speed of 100 words per minute doesn't demand our full attention, so we tune out the speaker and think of other things. We think of other things, and periodically we check back in with the speaker to see if anything interesting is going on. If we become more interested in what we are thinking of than in what the speaker is saying, it may be quite a while before we tune back in to what he's saying.

Everyone has a need to be listened to. What a wonderful service we provide, therefore, if we are good listeners. The manager who is a good listener fills a great need for every employee on the staff.

People pay large sums of money to be listened to by others—notably, by psychiatrists and psychologists. Some communities have established telephone "crisis lines" to help people with their problems. Some religious organizations have instituted prayer hot lines staffed by people who listen to callers and then pray with them. Further evidence of people's great need for listeners is the phenomenal growth of call-in radio shows, in which the caller's comments are aired live or on a delayed broadcast to a large listening audience.

Ego is another reason many people have trouble becoming good listeners. They have the mistaken notion that they are subjugating themselves to others by listening—that if they're not dominating the conversation, they're in an inferior position. Actually, the person doing the listening has more control than the talker. The talker desperately needs the listener. The listener doesn't need the talker; there are millions of talkers to take his place. Listeners are in great demand; talkers are a dime a dozen.

The Good Listener

Good listeners possess several traits, all of which can be developed. For one thing, they encourage the other person to talk. When listeners do talk, they don't turn the conversation back to themselves. They continue the line of talk of the other person. They use certain phrases or gestures to signal to the talker that they are truly interested in what she has to say.

Looking at someone who is talking to you indicates that you're interested in what he has to say—that, in fact, you are hanging on every word. Nodding your head affirmatively every once in a while indicates that you understand what the talker is saying. Smiling at the same time indicates that you are enjoying the conversation.

When discussing a problem with an employee, other thoughts are likely to enter your mind. You need to take control of those thoughts. While the person is discussing the problem, try to anticipate where the thought is going. What questions are likely to be asked? If someone is suggesting solutions to a problem, try to think of other solutions. Ideally, you'd like to focus 100 percent on what the person is saying, but the comprehension gap is a reality. By controlling your other thoughts, at least you can stay focused on the subject at hand, rather than on some extraneous idea that will be distracting.

A well-placed comment also indicates to the talker that you have a genuine interest in what he has to say.

"That's interesting."
"Tell me more."

"Why do you suppose she said that?"
"Why did you feel that way?"

As a matter of fact, just saying "That's interesting; tell me more" will make you a brilliant conversationalist in the minds of everyone with whom you come in contact.

Conversation Terminators

Once a manager achieves a reputation for being an outstanding listener, the staff lines up to discuss many matters. Some will overstay their welcome. They may even think talking to you beats working. You need to have some tools in your managerial toolbox to wind up these conversations.

The verbal conversational terminators are known to just about anyone who has held a job.

"I appreciate your coming in."
"It was nice talking to you."
"Let me think about that a while and get back to you."

There are also some more subtle conversation terminators that you may have seen. I bring them to your attention for two reasons: first, so that you can immediately recognize them when a more experienced executive uses them on you, and second, so you can use them when they seem appropriate.

If you've ever had a conversation in someone's office and, while you're talking, watched your host reach over and rest a hand on the telephone receiver even though the telephone hasn't rung, that's a conversation terminator. It says, "As soon as you leave, I'm going to make a phone call." Another technique is for the person to pick up a piece of paper from the desk and glance at it periodically during your conversation. By holding the paper in his hand, your host is saying, "I have something to take care of as soon as you depart."

The conversation terminator I particularly like is the one where the host turns in his chair behind the desk to a side position as though about to get up. If that doesn't work, he stands up. That always gets the message across. This approach seems too direct and I personally avoid it, but sometimes it becomes necessary.

Occasionally, you'll have an employee who is having such a good time visiting with you that all the signals are ignored. In that case, a verbal terminator that always works is, "I have really enjoyed the conversation, but I have work to do, and I'm sure you do, too." That is not rude for someone who has ignored all other invitations to depart.

It's important that you recognize these conversation terminators. You'll of course try to keep your conversations meaningful enough to preclude their use on you and your use of them on others. There are many more, but you'll compile your own list and find that different people have their own favorite conversation terminators.

Listening Summary

People enjoy being around someone who shows a genuine interest in them. Good listening skills carry over into many aspects of both your professional and personal life. The interesting thing is that you can start out using these techniques because you realize people will like being with you. There's nothing wrong with such an attitude. You become well liked and your subordinates get a manager who makes them feel good about themselves.

Everyone gains from such an arrangement. You may have to work on your human relations skills, but eventually they'll become second nature. At first you may consider such behavior to be role playing. But after a while you'll be unable to tell when the role playing has stopped and it's actually you. You'll derive a great deal of personal satisfaction from being the kind of person others enjoy being around. You'll also be a much more effective manager.

5

We, They, and My

"I don't know why *they* made that rule."

"*They* certainly don't understand how the people on the firing line feel."

"If *they* only knew how *we* feel about such practices."

"I don't know what *we* can do when *they* write such dumb memos and expect us to make them work."

Who are *they*? Who are *we*?

They is usually anyone who outranks you, although it may be anyone two levels above you. You are close to the people one level above you, and while they are suspect, you're not certain whose side they are on. *We* is anyone at your own level.

They and *we* vary depending on how you view the organization and yourself. To some members of *we*, you crossed the line into *they* the day you were promoted into management. As a manager you should avoid using the description of *they* for that nebulous group in control.

We're All in It Together

The function of everyone in management is to build the concept that the only group that exists is *we*. You may not change anyone but yourself, but isn't that where most worthwhile change starts—with one individual? It is a beginning toward putting your own thinking into proper perspective.

Many managers, at all levels, get into equal difficulty with another small word: *my*. Many new managers, and unfortunately many not so new, have the bad habit of using the possessive as it relates to staff. They say *"my* staff," *"my* department," *"my* assistant," and *"my* secretary."

Even if nothing is meant by this tendency, it is a bad one. It indicates ownership or a proprietary interest, and it is a tip-off of an improper attitude toward the people who report to you. You do not own the department, the assistant, or the secretary.

People reporting to you resent this phraseology, even though they may not feel free to tell you so. It's an indication of an ego problem on the part of the manager. During the Gulf War, I heard an Air Force general refer to aspects of the mission as "my planes" and "my plan." As a citizen and a taxpayer, I resented his attitude, and I can only guess at how a parent of one of those pilots would have reacted. I suspect it would have been: "He's not *your* pilot; he's *my* son." You can hear this attitude in management every day, and it is destructive of team building.

There are times when you cannot avoid such usage. If you're in a meeting with fellow managers and your boss, and the boss asks "How's the expense control in your department?" he's making an identification, not suggesting ownership. Likewise, there are other times when using the possessive avoids awkward or misleading statements. In this book, for instance, I refer to "your staff," or "your employees" for identification purposes only; it doesn't imply ownership. In these situations, the possessive is not an ego trip. But for the most part, try to avoid language that implies you own your staff.

A number of years ago, a friend told me that he'd had lunch with a mutual friend at the University Club. When I asked who it was, he mentioned my boss's name. I said, "Oh, I work for Jim."

"He never mentioned that," my friend replied. "He said that you were an associate of his. In fact, he mentioned that your office was right next door to his. He said he really enjoyed working with you."

He *was* my boss. His office *was* next to mine, and about twice as large. But he called me his "associate," and indicated he "enjoyed working" with me. That's not only completely free of ego but it's a class act. After all these years, the story still brings a smile to my face and a warm feeling toward my ex-boss.

Go and do likewise.

6

Change: Moving From Details to the Big Picture

In 1826, Ludwig Borne said, "Naught endures but change." To put that into today's language, it means, Nothing is as constant as change. How the manager handles aspects of change is covered in other sections of this book, but your overall attitude toward change is critical here. Change in this context means change for you: a move from detailed work to managing others.

The Manager's View of Change

Most people resist change. In an office, almost everyone wants things to stay the way they are. So it is no surprise that some new managers display a split personality when it comes to change. They are intolerant of any resistance to change by subordinates, but display the same resistance when faced with changing their own activities. Advancement into management is a form of change. You need to know what is involved and what qualities are required so you can make that change with grace and style.

Upward or Outward Change

Some bright managers look at the positions one step above them, and say to themselves, "Those people are my age, or younger. There is no opportunity for me in this company." They view the organization as static, and see no positive changes in their future. But this is seldom the case. People leave unexpectedly for a variety of reasons; others get promoted or advance through a reorganization. So instead of viewing your company as frozen in time, believe that if something can change, it probably will. Human beings are an unpredictable lot, and companies are peopled by unpredictable human beings.

From the Detailed to the General

As a part of management, you are now involved in the bigger picture. As a detail person, you probably handled only parts of an entire process, and you knew everything about that function. You had great *depth of know-how.*

There is now a shift in your know-how. There's less emphasis on your personal involvement in detail and more emphasis on the overall operation. This overall knowledge can be called *breadth of know-how.* As a person moves up the corporate ladder, this shift continues to evolve and the breadth of know-how expands while the depth diminishes.

A sports analogy makes the point. A football coach may have been a defensive lineman as a player. Now that he's the coach, he can no longer care only about the duties of a defensive lineman. He must now be concerned with all the position skills that constitute a successful team. If he has the occupational hobby of a defensive lineman, he may have a team with a great defense, but one that can't score points because it has no offensive capacity.

You must resist the temptation to make your old job your occupational hobby. That's often done because it's familiar and comfortable, but you must resist the temptation. Now you need to score points.

Pitfalls for the New Manager

Most first-time managers do not supervise a large group of people. Therefore, there may be a temptation to get too involved in the work of your six or seven people. As you move up the corporate ladder, you will be responsible for more and more workers. It is impossible to be involved in the detail work of thirty-five people, so begin now to distance yourself from the details of each task and concentrate on the overall project.

One of the dangers for a first-time manager is that you now may be managing someone who does your old job, and you may consider it more important than tasks you did not perform. It's human nature to think that what we do is more important than what others do, but that doesn't work when you're the manager. It is not a balanced approach to management.

Often, your first managerial job is a lead operator position. You manage others, but you still have tasks of your own to perform; you wear two hats. If this is your situation, you must stay interested and involved in the detail for a while. But when you move into a full-time management position, don't take an occupational hobby with you, lest it distract you from the bigger picture.

Of course, don't carry this advice to the extreme. When some people move into management, they refuse to help their staff at a "crunch and crisis" time. They read management journals while their staff is frantically meeting deadlines; they are now "in management." That is just plain stupid. You can build great rapport with your staff if, at crunch time, you roll up your sleeves and help resolve the crisis.

A Balanced Viewpoint

In all management matters, maintain a sense of balance. I have a friend who says, "I'm a big-picture guy; don't bother me with the details." But he says this when he's overlooked some serious element that is likely to impede the project at hand. He's joking, but many managers are not. They become so big-picture-oriented that they are oblivious to the details that bring the picture together. They also may be insensitive to how much effort is required to complete the detailed work.

Other managers, including many first-time managers who may have been promoted from a line position, are so enthralled with detail that the overall objective is lost. It's "not being able to see the forest for the trees." Balance is required.

7

Looking Above and Below

At my seminars I conduct a survey of the participants, based on the following chart:

I ask where the communication is best, and for the last two years, with few exceptions, attendees say it is best with their peers, second best with the boss, and third best with their own staff.

When I probe to find out why this is so, it is because people are more comfortable and feel nonthreatened with their peers than with their boss or their own staff. This reaction is absolutely backward. Your staff has more control over your future than do your peers or even your boss. Communication ought to be good at all levels, but if there is any ranking, the order ought to be: (1) your staff, (2) your boss, and (3) your peers. Peers have less to do with your future than the staff or your boss.

The reason for this preferred ranking is that your staff has the most impact upon your future. If the performance of your area is poor, no boss—no matter how well you are liked—is going to promote you. She can't defend it, and it will reflect badly upon her. Therefore the communication with your staff ought to be the best because open communication between you and your staff will enhance performance. The better the performance, the brighter the reflection upon you as manager.

In the two years I've been conducting this survey, I've yet to have a majority of attendees say that communication is best with their own staffs. People are communicating where they are comfortable, not where the payoff is greatest. Why are they not comfortable communicating with their own staffs? Is it possible that these managers are still caught up in "we and they"? Is it possible that the staff is now considered "they"? Isn't better communication the best opportunity to convert both the manager and the staff into one team—now appropriately entitled "we"? The communication needs to begin, and repeated over and over until the manager is completely comfortable with it.

Genuine Concern

One way to perform your job well is to give full attention to the needs of the people in your area of responsibility. Some leaders make the mistake of thinking that the concern they show for their subordinates will be interpreted as a sign of weakness. Genuine concern, indeed, is a sure sign of strength. Showing interest in the welfare of your people doesn't mean you'll "cave in" to unreasonable demands. Unfortunately, many new executives fail to recognize this. They're unable to differentiate between concern and weakness.

Your concern must of course be genuine. You can't fake it. By genuine concern I mean seeing that your people are properly challenged, and that they're appropriately rewarded when they perform well.

You can't start off by complacently telling yourself, "I'm going to be Mr. Nice Guy." You must seriously take on the burden of responsibility for these people. In fact, you and your team are mutually responsible to one another. Your subordinates now look to you for leadership. You must see to it that the objectives of the company and the objectives of your subordinates are not at cross-purposes. Your people should realize that they can achieve their own objectives only by doing their part in helping the company achieve its overall goals.

The person they look to for leadership is you. You serve as interpreter for the employees. What is the company's policy? You'd better be certain that you know what it is!

Showing Fairness

Another of your responsibilities is to make sure that work in your area is fairly and properly distributed so that no one is being carried along by the others or is doing more than a reasonable share of the carrying. In many offices, work assignments will vary; in others, nearly everyone will perform the same function. The supervisory task in the latter situation is much easier as far as equality of workload is concerned. It has other problems, however, in that relationships among the employees are likely to be more strained. Too many of the people will then spend their time worrying about distribution of work down to a gnat's eyelid. You don't have to be that exact. Your approach should be equitable without being scientifically equal.

I think it's more interesting to manage a section (unit, division, department) in which a wide variety of tasks are performed. You'll receive a variety of questions ranging from the routine clerical inquiry to the more complex professional one. The questions are important to the questioner, so you should give attention to all of them. You've probably seen the card in many executive offices: "Go ahead and ask your dumb question. It's easier to handle than a dumb mistake."

Variety Among Your Subordinates

You'll find people in your area who aren't interested in promotion. One reason is that they don't want to be responsible for the actions of others. Such people, however, might be interested in being promoted if the new position doesn't require supervising others. Many employees want to be responsible only for themselves, and their kind of personality is also needed in business and industry. The business environment would be rather chaotic if everyone were highly oriented toward managing everyone else.

In dealing with people who prefer not to work closely with anyone else, by all means put them in situations where their performance depends only on themselves. Some people are loners all the way. Then there are the *work loners,* who want to be left alone when it comes to the job but who are not necessarily antisocial. They'll go for coffee with their co-workers, have lunch with them, and even see them socially away from the office. Many workers respond best to the team approach. They need to feel they're part of a unit, and they'll develop great loyalty to their team. They'll perform well if you can put them into a team situation.

It's obvious that you can't get everyone into the ideal situation, but knowing that different people have different approaches to their work will make you a more effective manager. In other words, get people into situations where they're comfortable and you'll get a better performance from them.

Dealing With Your Superiors

I've spent some time talking about your attitude toward your subordinates; it's only proper to pay attention also to your attitude toward your superiors. Your future success indeed depends more on your subordinates than on your superiors, but it would be disastrous to ignore those who outrank you.

If you've just had a big promotion, you're feeling grateful to your boss. You're also pleased that the top exec was perceptive enough to have recognized the talent you have. But your new responsibility demands a new level of loyalty from you. After all, you're now a part of the management team. You can't be a good team member without identifying with the team.

Remember, however, that someone who is your superior in the company isn't necessarily smarter than you. Your boss may be more experienced than you, may have been with the company longer, may have come from the right family, or may be in the top position for other reasons. But it's also possible that your boss performed exceedingly well and is indeed smarter than you.

Loyalty to Them

Loyalty has fallen into widespread disrepute. Blind loyalty has never had much to recommend it, but being loyal doesn't mean selling your soul to the devil. Your company and your boss are not out to rip off the world. If they are, they're not worth being loyal to. More important, you shouldn't be working for them.

So let's assume you're convinced that your company's purpose is commendable and you're pleased to be associated with its goals. The kind of loyalty we're talking about has to do with carrying out policies or decisions you morally support. Your position with your company, let's again assume, allows you some input into decisions having to do with your own area of responsibility. You must make every effort to see that such input is as thoughtful and as broadly based as possible. Don't be the kind of narrow-sighted executive whose recommendations are designed to benefit only his or her own area of responsibility. When this happens, it won't be long before your advice isn't sought because it's too parochial.

If you make recommendations that are broadly based and represent the greater good of the company, your advice will be sought more often. This doesn't mean you're continually offering up your own people as sacrificial lambs. Keep everything in balance. The important thing is your involvement in the decision-making process beyond your own managerial level.

Occasionally a decision or policy will be made that's directly contrary to the opinions you've expressed; you'll be expected to support that decision or policy, and you may even have to implement it. Ask your boss why the decision was made, if you don't already know. Find out what important considerations went into formulation of the policy. Determine what you can about the processes that led to the decision.

The old idea that you follow the leader blindly no longer holds. That kind of loyalty was common during the Great Depression, when jobs were scarce and everyone who held a job wanted desperately to keep it. You can no longer bark orders and expect others to obey without question. We should be grateful that this approach no longer applies because today's more democratic approach requires people to be better managers. Nonetheless many managers and supervisors doubtless wish blind loyalty still existed.

If you're to do an outstanding job of supervision, you have a right to understand the reasons behind major company decisions and company policy. Perhaps your own manager is one who follows higher authority blindly and guards information about top management as if all of it were top secret—and you're the enemy. In that case you may have to be a lot more political in how you go about getting the answers to your questions.

If it's a policy that affects other departments, you can find out from people at your own organizational level in those departments. If a friend in Department X has a boss who shares information freely with subordinates, it may be relatively simple to find out what you want to know over a cup of coffee with your friend.

Dealing With an Unreasonable Boss

We do not live in a perfect world and as a result, some time in your career, you may be in the uncomfortable position of reporting to a difficult executive—someone who is also unpleasant to be around. Unfortunately, you can't fire an incompetent or unreasonable boss, as pleasant as that prospect might be.

Let's be quite candid. If a long-term executive is unreasonable, you have to wonder why the situation is allowed to exist. If everyone in the organization knows he's miserable to work for, why does top management allow the situation to continue? Top management cannot pull a Pontius Pilate routine and wash their hands of the situation. If top management doesn't know it, that's equally bad. What other intolerable situations are unknown in the executive suite? Enlightened executives do not believe in the mistreatment of any staff. The old-time attitude of "I don't care how you get the job done; just get it done" is archaic and opens the organization to a multitude of problems, including the ultimate survival of the company.

On the other hand, if everyone else in the department thinks the executive is a "good guy" and you're the only one having a problem, it's a far different situation. You may need to seek a conference with the executive to find out what the problem is, in his opinion. If you're fairly new to the department, you might give it some time by not reacting too quickly. The problem may solve itself if you do a great job and you are not hypersensitive. You may find it is style and not substance.

It is true that there are still too many companies that take advantage of a downturn in the economy to drive their people harder, recognizing that it's more difficult for people to leave. There are reasons why such an attitude is shortsighted. First, top-flight people can always find other jobs, no matter how tough the economy. It's the lesser talented people who cannot. So, this maladjusted company attitude drives away the more talented and retains the less talented. That's a recipe for mediocrity. Second, in a tough economy, appreciating all of your staff, including the very talented managers, places the organization in a stronger position to effectively compete. A company with a talented and appreciated staff will beat the brains out of a company that treats its employees merely as units of production. The long-range prospects for the latter style are not good.

An experience I had at one of my seminars puts this matter in some perspective. We were about two hours into a seminar for new managers and those who aspire to management. I noticed a young man at the end of one of the tables. I guessed him to be in his thirties. There was a set to his jaw and a look on his face that indicated he might not be buying into this humane management approach I was teaching.

At the first coffee break, I worked my way over to him and engaged him in small talk. After a few minutes, he said, "I think I agree with much of what you're saying. But I can't wait until I become a supervisor so that I can kick butt and rub people's noses into it the way I've had to take it these past years."

My response was, "That's great. You're going to continue a management style you hate. You'll get even with people who had nothing to do with your mistreatment. When does it end? Why don't you say, 'let it end with me' "?

The lesson of the unreasonable boss is to be the kind of leader you wish you had.

At the end of the day, the young man stood in his place, looking at me carrying on conversations with some of the departing attendees. When they left, he slowly walked up to me, shook my hand, and said "I don't know if I can do it your way, but I'll give it a try." That's all I can ask.

So if you are working for an unreasonable boss, do humanity a favor, and say, "let it end with me."

8

The Informal Organization Chart

Executives who have been around their companies a while will agree that there are two kinds of organization charts. The first is the one printed in the employee handbooks and perhaps the annual statements. That's the formal organization chart.

The other organization chart, which is never printed but is well known, is the way things really get done. As a first-time manager, you need to become well acquainted with the informal organization chart so you can increase the productivity of your staff and yourself.

One reason the informal organization chart is never drawn and printed is that it's doubtful every one knows all parts of it.

If you're new to the area you're managing, long-term employees will know how to get special jobs done quickly without going through channels. Tap into it. In my early days in management, I found one of the great sources for getting things done was to talk to secretaries. (Most are now called executive assistants.) These secretaries knew where to go to get certain tasks done quickly and accurately. If you don't have these channels you will waste much time and spin many wheels going through official channels. The objective is to get the job done, and often the official organization chart gets in the way of that objective.

Some enlightened executives might admit that they don't

know how to get everything done, but they know whom to ask to get it done. The result is the same.

Don't stand on formality; tap into the informal organization chart.

The Upside–Down Organization Chart

When you look at an organization chart, you usually find the board of directors at the top, followed by the executive officers, the junior officers, the middle managers, the first-line managers, and finally the people who actually do the work. Somewhere in that chart there will be various dotted lines, perhaps to staff support positions.

From an importance point of view, however, most organization charts are upside down, especially when management is perceived by the people who do the work.

Here's the way it should look from an importance point of view:

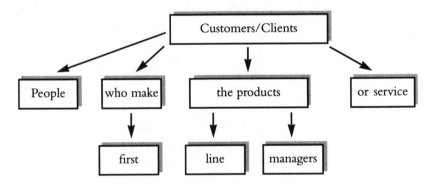

Without your customers, clients, or people you serve, there is no need for the organization. You have only the people who make the product or provide the basic service.

When you get beyond the first-line managers, you basically have *managers managing managers*. The primary place where workers being supervised meet management is at the first-line managerial level. This is where the management rubber meets the road.

The importance of the first-line manager cannot be overstated. The worker's view of management is primarily determined by how this first-line manager performs. To the worker, that person *is* company management. The relationship has a synergistic impact, either positively or negatively. With this importance in mind, one wonders how "swim or sink" can still be a major part of training—or rather, lack of training.

I don't believe companies will start turning their organization charts upside down, but wouldn't the symbolism be positive if the customer was at the top of the chart instead of at the bottom? After the customer, the future of the organization lies in the people doing the work and the first-line managers leading them. That is a significantly more dynamic situation than what goes on in the boardroom.

9

Management Style/ Team Building

Management responsibilities carry with them a style of operating—how a manager deals with people and gets tasks done. That style can be autocratic or diplomatic.

The Autocrat vs. the Diplomat

It's hard to believe that we still see the old-fashioned autocrat in management. You have to wonder why this is so. Partly it has to do with the fact that so many managers are given no training. They are left to find their own way, so they begin acting as they think they should. They think in terms of being a "boss" rather than a "team leader." Autocrats also believe that if they take the softer approach, employees will then take advantage. It's as though the softer approach will be seen as a sign of weakness.

Another possibility is that it takes more time to be a team leader. These managers spend time with people explaining not only *what* is to be done but also *why* it's done. The boss type doesn't want to be bothered—It's "Do it because I said so." That is shortsighted because people do a better job when they not only understand what they're doing but also why they're doing it. The diplomat realizes that the more people understand of what and why, the better they perform.

The autocrat wants to make every decision and views her staff as making robotic responses to her commands. She pushes the buttons, they snap to, and it happens. The diplomat knows that the time spent up front, getting everybody involved, pays off with huge dividends down the road.

The autocrat engenders fear while the diplomat builds respect and even affection. The autocrat causes people to mutter under their breath "Someday, I'll get even with this S.O.B." The diplomat causes people to say "He respects us and cares for us. I'd walk the last mile for him. All he needs to do is ask."

The autocrat believes the diplomat is a wimp. The diplomat believes the autocrat is a dictator. The difference is that the autocrat uses authority constantly, while the diplomat is judicious in its display.

The people working for the autocrat believe they are working *for* someone. Those reporting to the diplomat believe they are working *with* someone.

Team Building

The diplomat builds the unit into a team. People are consulted about changes that affect them.

Let's consider a major policy change by the company. The diplomat will tell staff about it and hold meetings, soliciting input from the staff on how the changes should be implemented. People recognize that receiving conflicting input from the staff still helps the manager make the decision, and everyone needs to recognize that it's his call. People will respect the idea that their input was solicited and considered.

When I was chief of staff to a U.S. senator, my recommendations were often solicited by the senator. My advice was not always followed, but that made it no less valuable. It was part of the body of information that helped him arrive at his decision—his decision, not mine.

Here's the beauty of building a team: You end up with a staff of self-starters. People see what needs to be done and they do it. They don't wait to be told. They know that their manager has confidence in them. If you build this kind of team, the staff will not tolerate a slacker in the group, because the slacker drags down the entire department and that reflects badly on all of them and you. When you build a great team, you'll never find a group of people more loyal. They become protective of you as their leader. Let someone from another department say something negative about you, and they have your entire team to deal with.

Of course, there are many shadings of styles between the two extremes we are discussing here. The manager who is an autocrat, or who has those tendencies, cannot build a team. He doesn't like questions. He almost thinks of questions as a form of insubordination. On the other hand, the diplomat loves questions because they signify interest and dedication.

Here's what an autocratic manager said: "Who asked you? If I want any ideas from you, I'll ask for them, but don't hold your breath. Look, it's my way or the highway, and if you don't like it, don't let the door hit you as you leave." The autocrat is insecure. The diplomat is not, because she knows that she's not in this alone. She has an entire team to get the job done.

Two
The End of the Honeymoon

10

The Art of Appreciation

In my management seminars, I often ask for a simple show of hands to this question: How long has it been since you've heard something like this from your manager? "I want you to know how much I appreciate the great job you did on that special project last Friday. I realize you had to work some overtime on the weekend to get it done. You did a terrific job. I am grateful to you. This company is fortunate to have you as a part of the staff."

I then ask, "How many of you have heard something like that in the last twelve months?" A few hands go up. I then ask, "How many have heard something like that in the last five years?" A few hands will go up. Then I ask, "How many have never heard it?" Anywhere from 25 to 50 percent of those in the audience have never received this kind of appreciation from their managers. These are not mediocre employees. They are in the seminar because they have recently been promoted into management, or are about to be. It is sad that people who are doing a good job receive no appreciation from their leaders. I usually end this section of the seminar by saying, "Such appreciation is important to you. Therefore, when you manage, don't withhold it from those who deserve it."

To underscore this point, at a group of thirty attendees, the following two questions were asked:

1. What is the best example of enlightened management you've ever seen?
2. What is the worst example of management you've experienced?

It was no surprise to me that nearly all of the responses had to do with some form of appreciation either received or denied when the staffer felt it was deserved. What did surprise me was the depth of emotion displayed about the subject.

There was one answer I will never forget.

A young man recounted how he was asked to get in a pickup truck and drive fifty miles to an outlying facility to make an important repair. At 10:30 P.M., after he had just returned home, the phone rang. It was his supervisor. "I just called to make sure that you got home okay. It's kind of a bad night out there." The supervisor did not even ask about how the repair went, which indicated his complete confidence in the young man's ability. The manager inquired only about his safe return. The incident had taken place more than five years earlier, but to the young worker it was as fresh as though it had happened last night.

In a poll conducted by one of America's major companies, employees were asked to rank work attributes they considered important. The money being paid for the work performed was ranked sixth. What came in first, by a wide margin, was "a need to be appreciated for what I do."

If appreciation is important to you in your relationship with your manager, realize that it is equally important to the people you manage. When people deserve appreciation, do not withhold it. It does not cost a single dollar, but it is so much more valuable than money.

11

Changing the Employee

Some psychologists maintain that the only way people change is through a traumatic experience, a religious conversion, or brain surgery. Whether or not this assertion is true, it does point to the difficulty we encounter if we expect to make basic changes in someone's personality. It's like the woman who marries an alcoholic because she feels it's her mission in life to change him. She may indeed change him if she's a traumatic experience for him.

Basic personality doesn't really change. Making slovenly workers meticulous is probably going to be an impossible task. You can smooth out "minor bumps" in behavior and cause people to modify their actions on the job, but you probably can't create a permanent personality change.

Doing What Comes Naturally

Attempting to change people's personalities or natural traits will, at best, provide mixed results. It makes more sense to move individuals into situations where their natural inclinations mesh with the job requirements.

Let's assume you have an outgoing person, who never met a stranger and who thrives on interaction with other people. What will happen if you give this extrovert a job that requires hours of working alone with great attention to detail? You're going to witness this person being drawn back to the company of others. On the other hand, if you have a shy person, who enjoys working alone and receives satisfaction from accomplishing solitary tasks, who requires little interaction with others, what will happen if this person is made chairman of a task force of ten people? He'll be unhappy and out of his comfort zone.

Too many managers—not just first-time ones—believe that everyone should be able, by gritting their teeth and by sheer determination and personal will, to do most any function in the area. People have all kinds of personalities, hobbies, interests, and ambitions. While they may be able to do a reasonable job on any task you assign them, wouldn't it make more sense to place them in tasks that fit their demonstrated, natural characteristics?

Companies need all kinds of people, with various skills, likes, and dislikes. Too often people are moved through an organization in a rigid line of succession. In doing so, management may be moving people out of their comfort zone.

Managing the Nit-Picking Employee

The worst thing you can do to a nit-picking, detail-loving person is remove the detail. Companies need nit-pickers. They are the people who clean up after the "big-picture hotshots." To paraphrase a psychologist I know, "Show me a person with a lot of drive, and I'll show you a nit-picking perfectionist following behind and cleaning up the mess."

Managing the Lazy Employee

On the other hand, I'd like to recommend the practice of indulging the lazy employee. Before you think I've completely lost my mind, let me explain. The lazy employees I've known are ceaselessly on the lookout for easier ways to do things. People who enjoy detail and busywork are not going to find out ways to eliminate them—because that's their thing. Not so with the lazy employee, who'll work hard and long at finding an easier way to do the job.

If you provide me with industrious people who like fussing endlessly over minutiae, I'll never be able to reduce staff.

However, sprinkle my staff with a few lazy souls and eventually I'll be able to reduce the number of employees. As some people leave, I won't have to replace them. And I know well that one of the key lines going straight to upper management's heart is "reduce staff and cost."

Matching Employees' Personality Traits and Preferences to Their Assigned Tasks

Too many managers assume that everyone reporting to them lusts after their manager's job. It's not necessarily so. Some want the money and the title but not the responsibility that goes with them. When we are looking for someone to assign to a task, it's not just a matter of finding someone who might be able to perform the task. What skills, including personality traits, are required to maximize the results wanted? Knowing who would enjoy the task and who wouldn't is also a factor.

In order for a department to function well it needs a variety of skills and personalities. (Incidentally, office personalities blossom under a diplomatic manager and wither or go underground under the autocrat.) All of these personalities need to be melded into an effective team. A baseball team will not function well with nine first basemen. Melding these various personalities and traits into an effective team is one of the manager's primary tasks.

A Last Resort: Dismissal or Transfer

Not every employee you manage is going to be successful in his job. This may require transfer to another area or outright dismissal. It's a procedure we should spend some time developing. Too often, in large offices, managers unload their problem employees onto another department through the promotion route. When asked by the manager of that other department how the prospective promotee is performing in the current job, they're not completely candid in their reply. I think the only correct policy in this situation is to be completely candid. Someday you yourself may be looking at people in other departments as candidates for promotion into your own department, and your best guarantee of not getting someone else's rejects is never to deliver that kind of cheap shot yourself.

I actually had that happen to me once. After we had reviewed personnel department performance appraisals of people one level below the job we were attempting to fill in our division, we ended up with three likely candidates. As is customary, I called the supervisors of these candidates and got a glowing report about one in particular, a man. We promoted him to our department and he ended up being a complete disaster. We had to terminate him after a short period of time because he wasn't doing the job. I then confronted the person who had made the recommendation and asked for an explanation, never dreaming I had been mousetrapped. The answer I got was that the employee had not been satisfactory but might become so if given another opportunity. By not being candid, they tricked me into doing their dirty work for them.

There's of course a great temptation to pay back such a department in kind, but the solution is to make sure no one ever does that to you in the first place. Retaliation in an intercompany operation is not beneficial to anyone.

Rehabilitation

There'd be nothing wrong, however, in attempting to rehabilitate a nonproductive employee if it were done with the full knowledge of everyone involved. In the situation where I was victimized, for example, had my fellow manager sat down with me and indicated that the employee was not doing a good job *but* there were strong reasons for wanting him to have another chance, I might have taken the man. I've known of such trials that have been successful. The work and the worker were not a good fit, but the worker had talent; the move to another area where that talent could be used turned a less than satisfactory employee into a productive one.

Generally, however, you'll be much more effective as a leader if you can solve your own problems in your own department and not unload them onto another department.

Companies use many testing devices to put people on jobs that are natural for them, or at least to place them in working areas of some personal preference. These devices range from simple five-minute tests to complex three-hour psychological evaluations. This is something your company either already has or should consider having. To emphasize my point again, you must always be conscious of the advantages of fitting employees to jobs at which they have the best chance of being successful. It's much easier to move people around into jobs that are natural for them than to force them into jobs they perform poorly and then try to "educate" them. It just doesn't work. Some psychologists think major changes in our personalities are unlikely to occur after age 16.

Serious Personal Problems

Some subordinates have personal problems that hinder their attendance and their performance on the job. You would be quite naïve to believe that alcohol, drugs, or serious family difficulties were not going to affect your management responsibilities.

Just because you're a manager doesn't mean you're equipped to handle every problem that comes your way. Many enlightened companies recognize this fact and have established employee assistance programs. These programs are usually community supported, unless the company is large enough to justify an on-site service. Employee assistance programs have professional resources available, have connections with chemical dependency programs, and know all the services that exist within the community.

It's foolish for you as a manager to believe that you have the capacity and the resources to solve any and all problems. If you try to handle a situation beyond your professional competence, you run the risk of making the situation worse. Amateurs have failed for years in dealing with alcoholics. As a manager, your responsibility is to see that the job gets done within the boundaries of sound management principles. The employee's alcohol or drug problem is interfering with accomplishing that objective. Although rescuing a human being is also a legitimate objective, you're swimming in uncharted waters.

You will probably need to have a direct confrontation with the problem employee, but you will have to define your *overall* objective first. Your objective is to straighten out a "work problem." You need to insist that troubled employees solve their problem, and you can even direct them to the employee assistance program. You have to make it clear that if they choose not to solve the problem, they will be dismissed from employment. Take care not to do this in a cruel, uncaring way, but be sure to be firm so there is no misunderstanding. People who are hooked on alcohol or drugs can be the greatest con artists in the world. They'll fake you right out of your socks if you're not careful.

You must be willing to listen, but not to the extent that problem employees spend a great deal of time in your office talking when they should be working. There's a fine line between being a good listener and allowing people to get away from their work for two hours while they drink coffee and pour out all their problems to you.

I don't mean to imply that alcohol and drugs are the only kinds of personal problems you will encounter. Sooner or later in your management career you'll hear of every conceivable problem (including inconceivable problems). People are involved in the totality of life; they have problems with spouses, children, parents, lovers, co-workers, themselves, religion, diets, feelings of self-worth, and so on.

A cardinal rule in dealing with human frailties, one that will save you endless aggravation, is *don't pass judgment*. Solve the work problem, and point employees to where they can solve their personal problems. In some cases you may demand that they solve the problem because of what the failure to find a solution is doing to the work environment.

Don't pass judgment and life will remain worth living.

Individual Style: Benefits and Detriments

Whenever possible, allow your subordinates to individualize the job as much as they can while still maintaining the quality, quantity, and objectives that have to be maintained to achieve company goals. The more you can allow your people to bring their own personality into the job, the better the chance of their being successful at it. The higher the position on the organization chart, the greater the latitude usually allowed for individual styling of that position.

Although it's important that you allow your subordinates to mold the job to their own personality, you have to keep them from riding their own occupational hobbyhorses. Some people will put an overwhelming emphasis on things they like to do, but these may not represent your own priorities in that particular situation. In every job, certain tasks are more important than others. As long as you and the employee agree about the relative importance of certain tasks and attend to them in that order of priority, you won't have a problem. You will have a problem when tasks you consider important are considered unimportant by the employee. You're then working in the reverse order of importance called for by the job. Too often we do the things we like to do first and continually put off doing disagreeable tasks. But in business the supervisor's order of priority always takes precedence over an employee's. Chapter 26, "Organizing Your Own Time," may be helpful in clarifying these matters.

Priorities

One of the biggest errors executives make is in not letting their employees know what work is considered the most important from the company's point of view. They take the attitude that it's all important. That puts employees in the position of deciding what should be done at what time. You can't then blame your subordinates if their sense of priorities ends up different from your own. You must discuss the situation with each employee, and of course the best time to have such a discussion is when the employee first moves into the job.

Subtle shifts repeatedly occur in defining the work load and its importance; to keep your sense of priorities up to date, you have to make sure you and your subordinates are constantly on the same wavelength.

It has often been said that people resist change. That's generally true, but a more precise statement is that people resist change when it's introduced too rapidly. If you can introduce change gradually, your people will accept it. In completely changing the rules so that it appears there's been a radical redefinition of the job, you're asking for real trouble unless the employees understand the reason for the change. They're being told to move out of their comfort zone; every habit they've formed and every bit of training they've received is being completely ignored. Most operational changes can and should be introduced gradually. In the few cases where they have to be introduced radically, perhaps overnight, you have no choice. You must then absolutely and thoroughly explain the necessity for the change.

Managing Change

All of us make changes in our work habits and in our personality, but they're so gradual that we never recognize them as change. Take a woman who worked on a particular job ten years ago; bring her back to the workplace today, she'll be amazed by the changes that have occurred in the job. A fellow worker who has remained on the job throughout those years, however, will be virtually unaware of the changes—*if* they were all introduced on a gradual basis. The more accurate statement, therefore, is that people resist uncomfortable change. Make the change comfortable for them by introducing it in small increments, and they won't fight you as severely.

What people say about change and the attitudes they display toward it are often quite different. A lot of people say "I just love variety," but watch them on the job and it's obvious that they're most content when working in what has been described as their comfort zone. The reason for this contradiction is that it's socially acceptable to want variety in a job, whereas it's not socially acceptable to be rigid or inflexible. Thus, even people who are rigid and inflexible will seldom admit it. Similarly, society is so oriented toward maintaining good human relations that we all claim to like working with people. A lot of us in fact prefer to work alone, but we don't say so because it's not socially acceptable not to enjoy working with people.

12

The In-Betweener

I wish someone had told me about the "in-betweener" when I was first promoted into management. It would have saved me much aggravation. I soon discovered that the in-betweener consumes an inordinate amount of the manager's time.

An *in-betweener* can be defined as an employee whose performance is not bad enough to fire, but not good enough to satisfy you, and thereby is of little concern.

The in-betweener is a real source of frustration. The manager desires one of two results at opposite ends of the spectrum: Either improve enough that there is no concern, or deteriorate to the point that you can be fired so that someone else can be placed in the job who will be a success.

Oftentimes the in-betweener is a long-time employee, and this long tenure makes it virtually impossible to dismiss the staffer. This situation probably could have been solved in the first year of employment. Marginal performance in the first year needs to be dealt with. If the person isn't cutting it in the first year, it can be for a variety of reasons, including selection, training, or lack of ability. When a marginal employee is allowed to remain a good number of years, he is likely to develop into an in-betweener. When someone does not do that managerial job in the first year, the situation stops being an employee fault and now is a company responsibility. You can't very well terminate a twenty-year in-betweener when the company allowed the situation to exist for nineteen years after the facts were known.

The in-betweener might be transferred to another area if

there is a position the employee might handle with a bit more competence. But the transfer approach requires the cooperation and complete knowledge of the other department. You must never unload your problems on another manager, as tempting as that prospect might be.

In one of my early managerial positions, I managed forty-seven people, which included three section supervisors who assisted with the leadership. Out of these forty-seven, I had five in-betweeners, all of whom had more than twenty years' tenure and all of whom were in the department when I was made manager. I spent more management time with those five people than I did the other forty-two combined. The time was spent in attempting to move them from borderline adequate to barely satisfactory performance. It was like a teeter-totter—up and down, down and up.

The in-betweener is one of those situations that a manager has to accept. You are not a god, and you cannot solve every human and every management problem. You're a manager, not a wizard.

13

Disciplining the Employee

Performance standards vary by the kind of business you are in, and may even vary by departments within the same company, because of the variety of tasks involved.

Every employee you are managing must know what work standards are expected. You create nasty problems for yourself when you discipline an employee on the basis of vague work standards. (It's like the way some people describe a tasteless movie: "Well, I can't define it, but I know it when I see it.") You can't get by with a nebulous approach to performance standards.

Having a desk manual for every job is an approach that many organizations use. There are books on how to write a desk manual. That subject is beyond the scope of this book, but basically a manual should describe the duties of the job, give some directions on how to do the job, and spell out some performance standards. One of the useful by-products of a desk manual is as a good cross-training device. It softens the panic that might otherwise set in when a key employee is out with the flu. Every position in your area of responsibility should be cross-trained.

Let's assume you've done a satisfactory job of establishing standards for each job. In all probability those standards are written into a job description. The job description indicates the elements of accountability that apply to the job; you can therefore measure the individual against those standards. Now you must have methods within your area of responsibility that allow you to be constantly aware of how people are performing in relationship to the standards. You can't operate on the assumption that unless you're hearing complaints from customers, or other departments, the performance is acceptable. By the time such warning signals arrive, severe damage may already have been done.

Prior Knowledge

Your own attitude about performance is crucial. The place and time for conveying your attitude about performance to employees is when they first step into the job. They need to know exactly what's expected of them. Performance standards will change. During the training period you'll accept less in the way of quality and quantity than afterward. You should have this properly backstopped during the training period so that the trainee's errors don't get beyond your own department.

Feedback is critical to proper and effective discipline. You must know as soon as possible when performance is substandard so that it can be corrected immediately. In the following discussion of discipline procedures, let's assume that you've set adequate standards and that the employee knows what those standards are. Further, you have an adequate method of feedback so that you know when substandard performance is a problem.

Never Make It Personal

One of the oldest rules of management is that employee discipline should always be done in private. Never humiliate an employee, even in cases of dismissal. The employee must always be made to understand that what is being discussed is the performance, not the person.

Too many managers, at all levels of experience, turn a discussion of poor performance into a personal attack. I don't think it's done maliciously. I suspect the approach is simply not thought through.

Here are some opening gambits that get the discussion off to a terrible start:

> "You are making far too many errors."
> "I don't know what your problem is. I've never had anyone screw up on this job like you."
> "Your performance is so substandard that we don't have an adjective to describe it."

These are outrageous statements, but attacks like these are uttered every working day somewhere. The managers may feel that they are right on target, but they have just made their problems worse than they need be.

Employees feel that they are being personally attacked. When attacked, our natural tendency is to defend ourselves, and the defensive barriers of these employees go up. Now both parties to the conversation have to fight through these barriers to get back to the problem. Give employees the benefit of the doubt. You might say, "I know you are concerned about the quality of the work at your desk." Attack the substandard performance by viewing it as the result of some misunderstanding about how the work should be done. Perhaps the employee has missed something in the training process, and this has created a systems deficiency that's causing the work to fall below the company's standards. By taking this approach, you inform the employee from the outset that you're talking about the performance and not the person.

Give and Take

You should have a conversation, not deliver a monologue. Many managers do all of the talking, meanwhile building up resentment in the party on the receiving end. You need to encourage the employee's participation in the conversation. Without it there's a good chance you won't solve the problem.

Be careful, now, and don't go overboard! Some executives, in their effort to be scrupulously fair, become so cautious and tactful that the employee leaves their office expecting to get a raise for outstanding performance. You have to make certain that your subordinate understands that the work is not up to standards. How you say it, though, is critically important.

When bringing the employee into your office, put him or her at ease. This may not seem like a big thing to you, but to an employee who doesn't often enter the sanctum of the high and mighty, you're the boss and being called into your presence may be a frightening prospect. Therefore, do everything you can to make the other comfortable.

Encourage the employee to participate in the discussion early in the game. You might start off with a statement like this: "Fred, you've been with us three months now and I think it's time we had a conversation about how you're getting along. As you know, I have a great interest in your being successful on this job. How do you feel things are going?"

By using this approach, you encourage an employee who is not performing up to standards to bring up the subject. It seldom comes as a surprise to an employee to learn that specified standards are not being met. Surprise is likely only if the employee has never been told what is expected. If that's the case, you really have some serious problems—problems of training and communication.

As the employee describes how things are going, you direct the conversation to the standards that are not being met. For example, you ask, "Do you think you're getting close to the standards we've established for experienced employees?" If the answer is yes, you could ask, "Do you believe you're performing at the same level as an experienced employee?" If the answer is again yes, then the employee may be out of touch with reality. The point is to continue asking questions of this type until you get the kind of response that will lead you into discussion of the quality of the work.

Obviously, if all your tactful efforts have failed to induce the employee to bring up the crucial subject, then you have no choice but to insert it into the conversation yourself. To the employee who persists in asserting that things are going well, you could say, "That's an interesting observation you've made about the quality of the work, because my observation indicates that it's not up to the standards we've set for the job. Why do you suppose my information is different from yours?" You then have the matter out on the desk for discussion.

Eliminate Misunderstanding

As you proceed further into the conversation, you use techniques that ensure that the employee knows what's expected. It's a good idea to get feedback on what you've mutually agreed upon, so there can be no misunderstanding later about what was said.

One way to make certain of this is to write a memorandum at the conclusion of the conversation and place it in the employee's file. This becomes particularly important if you're managing a lot of people and it's possible that six months from now you won't remember the details of the conversation.

The Primacy of the Person

There are problems about an employee's performance that cannot be separated from the person. When talking about the quality or quantity of an employee's work, it's obvious that the techniques I've just discussed can help in establishing firmly in the employee's mind that a difference exists between your criticism of the work and your view of the person. But with certain attitudinal problems it's more difficult to make the distinction, and in many cases it can't be done.

Let's assume you have a highly satisfactory employee who can't seem to get to work on time. Disciplining unsatisfactory employees is easier than disciplining a problem employee like this one whom you obviously want to keep. What happens in such situations is that if you allow the employee the privilege of coming in late every day, you're going to create a morale problem with the rest of the people who adhere to the office hours, no matter how superior that person's performance is. (What I'm saying obviously does not apply if your office has flexible working hours.)

In talking with the satisfactory employee about this problem, one of the better approaches is to explain the management difficulties you'd have if every employee ignored the working hours. You couldn't tolerate that situation. In addition, the employee is creating difficulties for himself. You can then go into the discussion in some detail and start working on a solution. Let's follow through with this problem of the tardy employee, because it happens often enough that you'll eventually have to face it.

Most conscientious employees who are doing a satisfactory job will react positively to your statements. You may notice that for the next ten days or so they appear at their desks on time. At that point you'll be feeling pretty smug about your success in managing people. You'll find, however, that when the pressure is off, the reformed employees will be coming in late again. You can't take a casual approach about this and assume it was just an unusual set of circumstances. All your subordinates must be made to know you expect them to be on time every day.

I would recommend that the first time this happens after your initial conversation, you again have a discussion with the offender. This doesn't have to be a full-blown dialogue of the same length and detail as the first one. All you need to do is reinforce what you said previously. There may have been a sound reason for the latest tardiness, and it could be that the second conversation will keep the employee on the straight and narrow. If you can get to the point where the employee is coming to work on time for approximately six months, you may assume you've changed that person's work patterns enough so that you no longer have a serious problem. What you should expect from that point on is the same attendance as you get from the rest of your employees.

Some Personal Experiences

I had something of this kind happen to me a number of years ago. The only difference from the situation just described is that this employee's performance was only slightly better than mediocre. I couldn't in clear conscience say the man was satisfactory. He was barely good enough to avoid being fired for incompetence. It got so bad that the people who worked around him nicknamed him "Sleepy." He really didn't come alive until about 10:00 A.M. I thought his first two tardinesses might have had just cause, but I became concerned when he volunteered no reason for being late. So on the third tardiness I had a talk with him and was told that he had difficulty getting started in the mornings. I sympathized with him, since I had the same problem. Because he was repeatedly arriving ten minutes late, I suggested he set the clocks in his house forward fifteen minutes. He said he'd try this, but he found that it didn't work. I then decided on a different approach.

I asked the employee if there was any physical reason for his having trouble getting started in the morning, perhaps anemia. He said that was not the case; he just was unable to get going in the morning. He had had this trouble all his life, through school and on his previous job.

The previous job had been in a small office where being on time was not considered critical. I then explained why it was important in the current situation, since the company employed a great number of people. In allowing one person to have a different starting time from all the rest, we created a problem as far as equitable treatment of employees was concerned. I then suggested the possibility of his going to bed earlier at night, and discovered the man was already sleeping twelve hours a night. I again told him it was very important that he solve the problem; in fact, his job depended on it.

I must admit that the situation did get better for about a week, but then the employee started slipping back into the old tardiness routine again. I need hardly add that the man had no trouble leaving on time at the end of the day. Following several further conversations with the offender, I ended by terminating him.

The situation just described is one that many executives would view as a failure of management skills. That's wrong. Not every personnel problem can be solved by accommodation. As far as I was concerned, I had done everything I could to remedy the situation, even to the point of suggesting that the employee visit his doctor for help. Since nothing I did worked, the only solution I had was to change to a new employee.

It's possible that you'll have other problems of a similar nature, such as spending too much time on coffee breaks, overstaying the lunch hour, or failing to be at the desk at a certain time. Needless to say, you don't run a sweatshop, and everyone will occasionally be tardy at some time or other. What's critical is dealing effectively with chronic offenders who create management problems for you and the organization.

Another difficult problem that you wouldn't expect in this day and age is cleanliness. This did happen to me once. The people working around the woman involved complained about the aroma emanating from her area. I avoided facing up to the problem because I was a new, young supervisor at the time and wasn't sure how to handle it. Eventually, I did face it and did have a conversation with the woman. She assured me that she bathed daily; we finally arrived at the joint conclusion that perhaps she wasn't getting her clothing dry-cleaned or washed as often as necessary to solve the problem. She did solve the problem, but left three months later, I think out of personal embarrassment.

If I had that one to handle over again, I believe I'd arrange to have someone in human resources talk directly to the employee rather than do it myself. The reason would not be to avoid a difficult situation, but rather to spare the woman embarrassment every time she saw me and the misery of being constantly reminded of the uncomfortable conversation. By having someone in human resources talk to her away from her work area, I might have solved the problem and also have been able to salvage an otherwise satisfactory employee. As it turned out, the woman moved out of town shortly after she quit, because her husband was transferred by his employer to another location, so I'd have lost her anyway.

Another situation that I recall along this line involved a man who was handling punch cards that were passed along from one area to another. I received a complaint because the man was always picking his ears and the person receiving the work from him didn't like handling soiled cards. I felt that the complaint might be legitimate; however, I decided against discussing it with the offender. Rather, I suggested to the man doing the complaining that he was perhaps being a little overly critical. I didn't say it in exactly that manner, but I let the man know that I didn't consider it quite as serious as he did. It was one of those problems that went away by itself.

This might be the place to make the observation that sometimes doing nothing is the right approach to solving a problem. But you have to be careful not to adopt a laissez-faire management attitude and assume that many problems will solve themselves.

The Disciplinary Approach

Getting to matters of greater seriousness, you might use a disciplinary approach in situations where you're attempting to correct performance. For example, you have a highly satisfactory employee whose work sharply deteriorates. Needless to say, you're continually communicating with the employee about the deterioration. You want to retain the employee, but you find that your words are not being taken seriously. In a situation like that you may recommend zero salary increase for the employee for that year, with a full explanation as to why you're doing it. Inform the employee in advance that if the work doesn't get better there'll be no increase in pay. Having made that threat or stated that possibility of action, you must then follow through on it so that you don't lose credibility. Some people don't actually believe you'll take such action. It's a technique that frequently works because people still care about the paycheck.

Another disciplinary technique you can use is to put the employee on probation. State that you have work deterioration that needs to be corrected and you want to give the employee every opportunity to correct it. You must make it perfectly clear that the substandard level of work being delivered cannot be allowed to continue. Also, you should set a deadline for a resolution to the problem. You might say to the employee, "This problem has to be solved within one month or we'll have to make other arrangements."

But first the employee must be made to understand exactly what kind of performance is being labeled substandard. The employee must also know how to correct it and must know what level of performance is expected. You mustn't arrive at the end of the probationary period only to find a legitimate difference of opinion as to how the employee is performing. The standards must be set so clearly that no disagreement about whether they've been met or not is possible. They must be measurable standards. You must keep a satisfactory set of records, because you may have to justify firing the employee if it comes to that.

Records are also helpful in raising performance standards. You can use the records to show your subordinates how they improved the quality of their work. This becomes an added gain because the employees are inspired to greater effort by pride in their accomplishment.

New employees in a company are often put on probation, either in line with standard company policy or as individual cases. You can't establish a probationary period for every employee in your department or division if it's not a company-wide practice. Many companies use a ninety-day probationary period. Employees doing satisfactory work at the end of that time are taken off the probationary rolls and become regular employees. It's also customary to give a modest salary increase in recognition of satisfactory completion of the probationary course. If the work is not satisfactory at that point, the employee should anticipate being terminated. Again, it should never come as a surprise.

Your Mood

People who report to you are very aware of what kind of mood you are in, especially if you tend to have wild mood swings. Temper tantrums have no place in the mature manager, and maturity has nothing to do with age. Letting your irritation show once in a while can be effective, as long as it is sincere and not manipulative.

All of us, from time to time at the office, fall under the spell of moods that reflect outside situations that are troubling us. Many books on management tell us we must leave our problems at the door, or at home, and not bring them into the office. I think that attitude is naïve, because few people can completely shut off a personal problem and keep it from affecting how they perform on the job.

There's no doubt, however, that you can minimize the impact a problem has on your work. The first step is to admit that something is irritating you and that it may affect your relationship with your co-workers. If you can do that, you can probably avoid making others victims of your personal problem. If an outside problem is gnawing at you and you have to deal with an employee in a critical situation, I see nothing wrong with saying to the employee, "Look, I'm really not in the greatest mood today. If I seem a little irritated, I hope you'll forgive me." This kind of candor is refreshing to a subordinate.

Never think for a moment that others don't have the ability to judge your moods. By showing dramatic changes of mood, you become less effective. In addition, your subordinates will know when to expect these changes, what the telltale signs are, and they'll avoid dealing with you when you're on the bottom swing of such a mood. They'll wait until you're on the high end of the pendulum.

Managing Your Feelings

You should work hard at being even-tempered. But I don't think it's a good idea to be the kind of manager who's bothered by nothing. I'm talking about the person who never seems to feel great joy, great sorrow, great anything. People will not identify with you if they believe you disguise all your feelings.

Keeping your cool all the time is another matter. There are good reasons for keeping your cool. If you can always remain fairly calm, even in troubled situations, you're more likely to think clearly and so be in a better position to handle tough problems. But it's also important that you show feelings once in a while, or people will think you're a management robot.

To be an outstanding manager of people, you have to care about people. That doesn't mean taking a missionary or social-worker approach toward them, but if you enjoy their company and respect their feelings, you'll be much more effective in your job than the supervisor who's mostly "thing" oriented.

This, indeed, is one of the problems companies bring on themselves when they assume that the most efficient worker in an area is the one who should be promoted to management. That worker may be efficient because of being "thing" oriented. Moving such "experts" into areas where they supervise others doesn't automatically make them "people" oriented.

14

Hiring and Training New Employees

There are probably as many different hiring practices as there are companies. If I were to attempt to cover all the various methods, I'd never get to the end of this chapter, so let's make a couple of simple assumptions. Let's say the human resources department does the initial screening but you have the ultimate decision-making authority as to who comes to work in your area of responsibility.

The Use of Tests

With greater federal, state, and sometimes city participation in hiring procedures, your company may not do much testing of prospective employees. I'm aware of one company that has done away with all such tests. Instead, it uses only what I call *posthiring tests* to fire people early in the game if they don't cut the mustard.

This is the most expensive method of testing I can think of. I suspect it's an overreaction to government involvement in hiring procedures. Companies may increasingly resort to this method as their frustration levels increase. In so doing they make the problems of management more difficult, not to mention the psychological damage done to people who are fired when their only mistake was in having been hired in the first place.

The quality of prospective employees will vary a great deal. When unemployment rates are high, you'll find greater interest being shown in the job and you'll have a larger number of prospects to choose from. The reverse will be true when unemployment rates are low. I've known situations where available employees were so few that you'd consider hiring anyone who appeared at your desk. So there'll be forces beyond your control. We're concerned here with situations you can control.

If tests are used by your human resources department, consider first those that are relevant to the position to be filled. Math aptitude may not be important if you're hiring for a typing or secretarial job; ability to spell would be more to the point.

The Missing Ingredient

Almost without exception, when I ask seminar attendees what is the most important ingredient in hiring a new employee, they come up with experience, qualification, or education. They rarely come up with the missing ingredient.

I suggest that the most important ingredient in hiring a new employee is *attitude*. You can hire an employee with all of the experience, education, and qualifications you could hope for, but if the person has a bad attitude, you have just hired a problem employee. On the other hand, you can hire a person with less experience, education, and qualifications, and if that person displays an outstanding attitude, in all likelihood you will have an outstanding employee. Every experienced manager will agree that attitude is the most important element in an employee.

The Screening Process

Most managers do too much talking and too little listening in the interviewing process.

The interview with the prospect is a two-way sizing up. Naturally, the prospect wants the job, so she will give you the answers she believes will maximize her chances. Any applicant who doesn't isn't bright enough to be hired.

Don't ask such difficult questions that the prospect can't possibly answer them. Here are some questions that managers who pride themselves on being tough interviewers might ask; and these should be avoided:

"Why do you want to work here?"
"What makes you think you're qualified for this job?"
"Are you interested in this job because of the salary?"

Dumb questions like these will make you a rotten interviewer. You must strive to put the prospect at ease so that you can carry on a conversation. Your aim is to know the prospect better, and that means avoiding a confrontation. Rather, make statements or ask questions that will relax the applicant. Hold the tougher questions—but not the three above—for later in the process. Consider the following sample interview.

Mrs. Valencia's Job Interview

The objective ought to be to find out if the applicant meets the job qualifications and *has a good attitude*. It makes some sense to spend the early part of the interview engaging the applicant in some nonthreatening small talk.

Most applicants are nervous. They have a lot riding on the results. The idea is to put the person at ease. By not immediately going to the business at hand, you let her know you're interested in her as a person, apart from the job. It's important that you develop a comfortable relationship. If this woman is going to work for you, it's the beginning of what could be years of daily contact. Even if she doesn't get the job, she'll feel more kindly toward you and your company because you've shown a sincere interest in her.

Note: A company has many "publics": the general public, the customers, the industry it is part of, government agencies that it comes in contact with, and your employees and those who apply to be. I know a woman who was a substantial patron of an upscale department store, who thought it would be fun to have a part-time job there. She resented the treatment she received when she applied for a job, and vowed never to set foot in the store again. That cost the store thousands of dollars a year from her purchases alone, not including the purchases all her friends would have made had she not shared her experience with them.

When the small talk is over, you might consider using this approach: "Mrs. Valencia, before we start talking specifically about the position you've applied for, I'd like to tell you a little about our company. Because, while we're considering you, you're also considering us, so we want to answer any questions you may have about our company."

Then go ahead and tell her something about the company. Tell her what your purpose is, but don't spend a lot of time on statistics. Talk more about the company's relationship with its employees. Tell her anything in this area that's unique. You want her to get a feel for the company and its people. This additional talk is to give her a feel for the company she wishes to be a part of, and it also gives her more opportunity to relax and feel comfortable.

We now arrive at the critical point in the interview. You want to ask questions that are going to give you some clues about this person's attitude. Most people-oriented managers (and that's most of them) cannot stand a vacuum, so if the applicant doesn't respond promptly, they tend to move in and try to help out. It's an act of kindness, but in this case it interferes with obtaining the crucial information you need to make a proper selection.

Some sample questions are:

"What did you like best about your last job?"
"What did you like least about your last job?"
"How did you feel about your last manager?"

These are sample questions. You might devise some of your own that seem more appropriate for you, but until you do you might consider the ones I've suggested.

Let's examine each question and what wrong and right answers can tip you off about employee attitude.

If the answer to question 1 mentions such items as the challenge of the job, the fact that the company promoted from within, that the company encouraged and assisted with educational opportunities, or that self-starters were appreciated, you have indications of someone who has recognized what is important in a sound working environment.

However, if her answers mention such things as the office being closed every other Friday, which made for nice long weekends, that the company provided many social activities, including both a bowling and a golf league, and that employees received a paid vacation the first year with the company, you may have an applicant who is looking for a place to socialize. This person may be a social butterfly, and while there's nothing wrong with enjoying the company of others, that should not be the main reason for seeking the job.

Now let's discuss some potential answers to question 2, about the items liked least on the last job. If the answer involves something like being required to work overtime occasionally, being asked to come in on a Saturday, or being expected to give up a Saturday to go to a community college for acquiring some skills that will be helpful on the job, even though the company paid the seminar fee, those are wrong answers.

However, if the answer mentions that the company had no formal performance appraisal system, that the granting of raises didn't seem to bear any relationship to quality, or that there wasn't anything the person really disliked, but just feels there might be better opportunities elsewhere, those are thoughtful, "burn no bridges" responses.

Let's now move to question 3. You'll note that the question is more open-ended. If the applicant really trashes her last supervisor, and is generally negative, such as, "I don't think I ought to use the kind of language it takes to describe the S.O.B." that is a negative answer.

Let's assume that the relationship with the last supervisor was terrible, but she answers, "Well, as with many bosses, we had our differences, but I liked and respected her." That is a diplomatic description of what may have been a bad situation.

You may also say to the applicant, "I've been asking you all these questions. Do you have any questions you'd like to ask of me?" The questions asked by the prospect can also provide clues to attitude.

What if questions from the prospect are along these lines?

"How many holidays do you close for each year?"
"How much vacation do you give the first year? How long do you have to be here to get four weeks vacation?"
"What social activities does the company sponsor for the employees?"
"What's the earliest age you can retire? How many years of service do you need?"

Questions along this path indicate someone who has an attitude focused on getting out of work rather than into it. My samples are obvious, and again overdrawn to make the point. Some questions asked by the applicant may be more subtle than this, but are still a tipoff of an undesirable attitude.

The following sample questions asked by applicants generate a decidedly different attitudinal bent:

"Are people promoted based on performance?"
"Can an outstanding performer receive a larger salary increase than an average performer?"
"Does the company have regular training programs for the employees, so they can broaden their work skills?"

The thought may have entered your mind that the applicant is giving you the answers she thinks you want to hear. If that is so, it indicates you are not interviewing a dummy. Isn't an employee who can anticipate what the answers ought to be going to be a better staffer than an applicant who hasn't a clue as to how to respond? A job prospect who trashes a former company or supervisor, even if deserved, says more about herself than about the object of scorn. There is no way such an approach will advance her prospects for the job, so the insightful person will avoid negative comments about past working relationships.

An important strategy the manager brings to the interview process is silence. When a person does not answer right away, the silence may feel uncomfortable but if you jump in, you are not as likely to get the same answer.

In this whole area of questions, I am assuming that the human resources department has oriented managers in the types of questions that can and cannot be asked. You need to know the areas that you cannot move into because they are discriminatory or illegal, or both.

One forbidden question that comes to mind is, "Do you have to provide child care for children?" Knowing that is one of the topics you cannot broach, if the applicant asks about work hours, do not consider that a negative question. It may be triggered by a concern about child care.

Another question from an applicant that should not be considered a negative has to do with health insurance. An employee asking about health benefits is showing responsibility. In short, it is the general tenor of questions that indicate an attitude problem. You have to use your good judgment about which subjects denote attitude and which indicate responsibility.

In describing a job, I usually include some basic information that everybody would like to have, so that they don't have to ask. I tell them the hours, the starting salary, the length of probationary period, and whether successful completion of that trial period generates a salary increase. I also include a brief overview of the benefits package. My reasoning is that by getting this basic information out of the way, I avoid cluttering up the open-ended questions that provided the attitude clues needed to make a hiring judgment.

As you obtain more experience with the interview process, you will become skilled at it. In most job interviews, employee attitude is completely ignored. Typically, the manager holds the application in her hand and says, "Well, I see you worked for the XYZ Company." Look that application over before you sit down with the applicant. Don't see it for the first time in the presence of the applicant. Then ask the questions that reveal work attitudes.

The Effects of Unemployment Rates

If your town has a high unemployment rate, you'll get better acting performances from prospective employees. (If you desperately needed steady work and a steady paycheck, you'd take almost any kind of job. You'd also be more adroit in selling the interviewer on why you should have the job.)

With high unemployment, you'll also run into overqualified applicants. Frankly, I have mixed emotions about these people. I strongly empathize with them in their current dilemma, but I also realize that once other opportunities open up, which make it possible for them to cash in on their full qualifications, you will lose these employees. The few times I have hired an obviously overqualified person I've ended up regretting it, for a couple of reasons. First, if the person is working below her capacity, she is not challenged in the job. Second, she is immediately looking for a better job.

Knowing the unwillingness of most managers to hire overqualified workers, some desperate applicants will shade their qualifications on the application, so that their greater education or experience is hidden. If you hire overqualified people, prepare to lose them.

The Comfort-Zone Underachiever

A comfort-zone underachiever (CZU) is a person who is highly qualified but doesn't like being challenged. There are a lot of them around, but very few of them admit it.

One of the main problems for CZUs is convincing you they genuinely want to work at a position that seems far below their capacity. They often get burned, in that they're not hired for jobs they want because they're overqualified. They soon discover that the way to handle this is not to list all their qualifications on the job application. The registered nurse who doesn't want to practice nursing may not indicate her training in that field. She may trim her list of qualifications to fit the clerical job she wants. Likewise, the schoolteacher who really can't stand young children in a classroom environment may not list all his credentials. Handling previous work experience on the job application gets more difficult because the trained interviewer will zero in on any gaps. So if our teacher really wants the job as the office "lawn man," his application might show him as a member of the school's "maintenance crew" rather than of its teaching staff.

Since you're interested in getting ahead and managing other people, you may have trouble understanding applicants with this kind of personality. Don't underestimate them. They certainly aren't stupid. They see work from a different perspective than you do. It isn't a matter of who's right and who's wrong. Each attitude is right for the people involved.

It's like the forty-five-year-old CZU dentist who despised the nineteen-year-old he once was because of the decision to spend the rest of his life looking into mouths and filling teeth. There are a lot of unhappy people working at unsuitable jobs and we should respect CZUs for having the courage to change their situation. People resist change, and the combination of resisting change and knowing change is necessary leads to inner emotional conflict. I believe that's what psychologists call avoidance—avoidance conflict: You're trapped by having to choose between two unpleasant alternatives because by doing nothing you're eating yourself alive.

The comfort-zone underachiever is trying to find "what's right for me." The job CZUs take may be temporary; they're at a crossroads in a period of reassessment. Often they're looking for a job that won't divert them from their search. The job will require a minimum of attention, thus freeing them to think, to sort things out. Often they'll go after a job that's highly repetitive in nature, that can be done accurately without effort, thus enabling them to daydream. Certain jobs in your own company would doubtless drive you bananas in two hours, but there are people who enjoy doing those jobs; it's a matter of the proper fit.

Work and Play

The word *work* has a bad image for many people. To them, work is a form of punishment. Perhaps it goes back to the ejection of Adam and Eve from the Garden of Eden. If they had not been driven out, they'd still have had to figure out a way to occupy themselves, but the activities would have been by choice and so would have been thought of as play rather than as work. If I play tennis for a living (in which case I'd starve to death), it's work; but if I play it for recreation, it's play. It's still tennis. Perhaps it comes down to a distinction between have-to and want-to situations. That's why many people who are independently wealthy still work. For them it's a want-to situation.

Describing the Job

Let's return to the sample interview with Mrs. Valencia. In talking with her about the job, describe it in nontechnical terms—use terms she'll understand. The jargon and acronyms of your business are commonplace to you, but they are a foreign language to new employees. The same situation exists with job descriptions. If they are written in technical jargon, they will mean very little to prospective employees.

Making the Hire

If you're considering several people for the job, be careful not to mislead any of the prospects. Tell them that a decision will not be made until all the prospects have been interviewed. They should appreciate the fairness of that arrangement. Tell them that they will be called as soon as a decision has been reached. See that they are phoned that day and informed of the decision.

I prefer that all prospects be phoned by the human resources department and told that a decision has been made. You might, of course, want to deliver the good news yourself and phone the person selected. This approach may make you a big shot with Mrs. Valencia, but it won't do a whole lot for your image with the human resources department: They handle the dirty work; you handle the good news. If they have to inform six people that they didn't get the job, at least let them deliver the good news to the one who is going to be hired.

The Attitude Talk

After the applicant is selected for the job, you should have your "attitude talk" with the person. Here's a summary of my version of an attitude talk; you'll develop your own style after a while, but the basic thoughts remain the same:

"One of the reasons you were selected for this position is that you display the kind of attitude we want in this organization. Your application and tests indicate that you have the capacity to handle the job. Many of the people who applied had the qualifications to do the job, but the one reason you were selected above all the others was that you display the kind of attitude we are looking for. We believe that the difference between an average employee and an outstanding one is often attitude. Not everyone in this organization has a great attitude. What do we mean by *attitude*? The attitude we're talking about is one where you are not worrying about whether you're doing more than your share. It's an attitude of pride in doing high-quality work and gaining a sense of accomplishment at day's end. It's personal satisfaction in a job well done. We believe you display that kind of attitude, and coupled with your ability to handle the job, you will make an outstanding addition to our organization."

Now let's analyze the reasons for some of the statements in this mini speech.

• When is an employee most likely to be receptive to ideas about the job? Isn't it at the start of a new position?

• Do people generally try to live up to the image they think you have of them? I think they do. Recall the interview and the possibility that the applicant may have been displaying the attitude she thought you wanted. She now knows that attitude is exceedingly important to the company and to you as her manager. She now needs to display such an attitude on the job. Isn't that a win-win situation for both her and the company? I think so.

• Why advertise the fact that there are people in the company who do not have a great attitude? Because of your own credibility. If you remain silent about some who may have an undesirable attitude, your words become hollow, indeed, when this new employee runs into one of them. However, since you mentioned it, now when she encounters a fellow employee with a bad attitude, your credibility is enhanced. She may think, "He told me there are some with a bad attitude like this. I'm here to help change it." Your credibility is fortified.

The exact moment for your attitude talk with a new employee is a matter of personal preference. I prefer bringing the person back into the office after she has been notified she got the job. That strikes me as an ideal time to congratulate the person and give the attitude talk. It should be reinforced the first day on the job too, but in a low-key way because there are so many things on the new employee's mind that day. She's nervous; she's concerned about how she's going to like the people she is going to meet and if they will like her. But that first day is when the new employee is most receptive to what is expected.

Your Attitude Toward Training

Many new managers believe they must know how to perform every job in their area of responsibility. It's as though they feel that if some key person quits, they might have to get out there and personally perform the task. If you believe in that philosophy and carry it to its logical conclusion, then the chief executive officer of the organization ought to be able to perform every job in the company. That of course is ridiculous. It's just as ridiculous as believing that the President of the United States should be able to perform every task in the federal government. The President shouldn't even be able to perform every job in the White House. You don't have to be a master chef to recognize rotten chicken.

You need to know what needs to be done, not exactly how it's done. A lot depends on what level manager you are. If you are what I call a performer-manager, you are responsible for doing some of the work yourself and leading others in the same function. In that set of circumstances you will know how to perform the operation.

However, if you have thirty-five people performing a variety of tasks, you will not know how to perform each task—but you will have someone out there (in addition to the basic operator) who does know how it's done. The administrator of a large hospital is not able to perform surgery, but that administrator knows the process by which skilled surgeons are secured and retained on the staff.

Many new managers are uncomfortable about what they can't do. Don't be. You're going to be held responsible for the results you achieve within the confines of company policy. You will not be responsible for crossing every *t* and dotting every *i* yourself.

Although this concept may be frightening to you at first, you'll get used to it and wonder how you could have ever thought otherwise. Your initial reaction will be, "I've got to know it all." If it's a big, varied operation, you can't possibly know it all. Don't sweat it.

Training the New Employee

In many ways, instructions given employees on their first day are wasted motion. Their first day on the job is an opportunity for new employees to get acquainted with the people they'll be working with and to find out where the rest rooms are. You should permit them to spend the first day just observing and then start the actual training the second day. Many workers go home from their first day on the job with either a bad headache or a backache—undoubtedly the result of nervous tension.

There are different philosophies on how a person should be trained. The most common philosophy holds that a new employee should be trained by the person leaving the job. Automatically following that philosophy can be a mistake.

Everything depends on why the employee is leaving and on her attitude.

The Wrong Way: An Example

Let me give an example of the wrong way to train a new employee. It demonstrates the worst kind of judgment I've ever seen displayed in this type of situation. The manager of an office consisting of several salespeople and one clerical person decided that the clerk should be fired for incompetence. He gave her two weeks' notice but asked her to work during that time. He then hired her replacement and asked her to train the new employee. The result was a nightmare for all concerned.

And no wonder! If the person leaving your company is less than 100 percent competent, you must never allow him to do the training. Most people who put in their notice don't "give a damn" from that point on. The training they do will be casual and incomplete. In addition, they may pass all their bad habits on to the new employee. On the other hand, when a position opens up because the incumbent in the job is being promoted, that person is probably the best one to handle the training.

Concerning the manager who wanted the fired employee to train the replacement, he did not himself understand the clerical job. It was impossible for him personally to train the new employee—any attempt to do so would merely have displayed his ignorance. He therefore went to impossible extremes to "keep his cover." That's a serious managerial failure.

But don't misconstrue what I've said to mean that a manager must personally know how to perform every job in the organization. I don't mean that at all. In the example given, however, there was only one clerical operation. If the manager didn't know that elementary job, how in the world could he effectively manage? The answer is he couldn't!

Managing the Small Office

I've known of situations in small offices with a single secretary and a couple of clerks where the manager takes the attitude

"You handle all of the office routine and the paperwork. I don't care how you do it as long as you get the job done and as long as you can find what I'm looking for."

I don't see how you can manage a small office that way. How do you measure the performance of your subordinate? What is your standard of measurement? Too often people told to do it their own way set out to make themselves indispensable and succeed in the effort.

Unfortunately, that kind of situation prevails in far too many small offices. The clerical staff becomes the office manager and develops systems no one else can figure out. That must not be allowed to occur. The executive in a small office must understand the systems and must forbid any system to develop that enhances the indispensability of subordinates. The system must be the company's and not the employees'.

A Solution: The Work Manual

Some companies solve this problem by putting together a work or desk manual that describes the basic office duties and how they're to be performed. Routine clerical positions lend themselves better to this treatment than more complicated tasks do. Jobs requiring judgment cannot easily be reduced to simple written instructions because all their contingencies cannot be anticipated.

Work manuals are fine if they're kept current. If they're not, they become worthless.

The Role of the Trainer

Before starting a new employee on a training course, you must have a talk with the prospective trainer. You should never spring it as a surprise. Once the new employee is hired and a starting date has been established, notify the person you've selected as the trainer. The trainer may have to rearrange some schedules to accommodate the assignment.

Pick a trainer who is very good at explaining what is going on—one who can break the job down into its component parts and who doesn't describe it in technical jargon. The jargon will be picked up eventually, but the trainee must not be overwhelmed by this "foreign language."

You must outline to the trainer what you want to happen. If you'd like the first day to be casual, the trainer needs to know that.

Sometime during the latter part of the first day, you should stop by and ask the trainer and the trainee how things are going. What you say is not as important as your display of interest in the new employee.

At the end of the first week, call the employee into the office for a chat. Again, what is said is not as important as the interest displayed in the new employee's welfare. Ask a couple of questions to determine if the instructions from the trainer are clear. Is the new employee beginning to get a handle on the job?

The Improvement Seed

This is also the time for planting the *improvement seed*. The process might take the form of this discussion with the employee:

"As a new person on this job, you bring fresh insights to the position that the rest of us may not have. After you've been at it a while, you may not be able to see the forest for the trees. I encourage you to ask any questions about what we do and why we do it. After you've been trained, we encourage you to offer any suggestions you can think of to improve what we're doing. Just because you're new doesn't mean your ideas are invalid. What seems obvious to you as a new employee may not be so obvious to the rest of us."

The reason for emphasizing "after you've been at it" is to keep new employees from suggesting changes before they understand what's going on. What may seem like a good idea early in the training may be taken care of as the nature of the position becomes more clearly understood.

Everyone you manage must know that you regularly do this improvement number. In that way, you make it less likely that they'll react negatively to new ideas.

You'll always have plenty of problems with people who defend themselves with the statement, "We've always done it this way." Such an argument is usually desperate; it tells you unmistakably that the person using it can't come up with a valid explanation of why something is being done.

The Job Defined

During the training period, it's a good idea to break the job down into small parts and teach the functions one at a time. In showing new employees the entire function, you run the risk of overwhelming them. You should, of course, explain the purpose of the job first.

Feedback

It's important to develop a method of feedback that lets you know how well the trainee is doing after beginning to work unassisted on the job. The trainee should take over the job from the trainer on a gradual basis as each step in the process is mastered. The feedback method should apply to every employee. The system should be developed in such a manner that unsatisfactory performance always comes to your attention before too much damage is done. The process is vital to your success as a manager, but no strict guidelines can be offered for establishing it because it will vary according to the line of business you're in.

The feedback must be internal. Hearing about the mistake from a dissatisfied client or customer means it's already too late. You want to correct the problem before the work gets out of your own area of responsibility.

Quality Control

If it's possible to maintain quality control procedures your employees can relate to, so much the better. Don't expect perfection; that's an unrealistic goal. Determine what an acceptable margin of error should be for your area and then strive as a team to reach that goal and eventually better it. The goal must be realistic if you expect the cooperation of your staff.

A baseball player batting .250 can make out extremely well in the major leagues. One batting .300—getting the job done three times out of ten—is now considered a superstar. You can't survive with that kind of percentage. Depending on what kind of business you're in, it's questionable that you could survive even with a 10 percent rate of error. Let's use a 5 percent rate of error for discussion purposes, even though it may not be realistic for your business.

New employees need to know what's expected of them once they're operating on the job alone. If your ultimate goal for them is 95 percent efficiency, it would help them if they knew what your interim targets are. You might expect them to be working at 70 percent efficiency at the end of thirty days, at 80 percent efficiency at the end of sixty days, and at 95 percent efficiency at the end of ninety days. This will depend on how difficult the work is. The simpler the job, the easier it should be to get to the ultimate quality goal. You have to determine the timetable and let the new employee know what it is.

Even when the new employees take over the job on their own, you should have the trainer audit their work until you believe the work is acceptable and quality checks are not so crucial.

Each mistake should be gone over carefully with the trainee. The trainer must be a diplomat. The trainer must talk about what went wrong and not attack the new employee. Don't make it personal. The trainer should not say, "You're making a mistake again." Rather, something like this might be more appropriate: "Well, this still is not 100 percent, but I think we're getting closer, don't you?"

End of the Training Period

At some point the probationary period must end. In most companies this is usually after a specified number of weeks or months. However, I believe that once the trainee demonstrates the ability to work unassisted, it's time for another formal interview between you and the trainee. This marks the completion of a phase in the new employee's career, and some attention should be paid to the event. All you really need do is express your satisfaction about the progress made up to this point, note that the employee will now be working on his or her own, and indicate how the work will be monitored both for quality and for quantity.

15

"Oh My God, I Can't Fire Anyone!"

If there's one moment that will live forever in a manager's memory, it's the first time a subordinate has to be fired. It's not a pleasant task. If you enjoy it, then I question your ability to manage people.

Firing someone can be traumatic for both parties in the drama. If you've done your job properly, the event will not come as a surprise to the person who is about to get the ax.

Sudden firings are nearly always wrong, except in cases where an employee has been dishonest or violent. Never fire someone when you're angry. Never take such radical action on an impulse. When a subordinate pushes you over the edge and you feel like "showing who's boss," don't give in to your emotions. If you do, you'll regret it.

As you read this chapter, the thought may occur to you that some people don't deserve the time and consideration I'm recommending. You may be right, but I believe in erring on the side of excess deliberation rather than on the side of excess haste. In fact, some managerial friends of mine adopt the philosophy of never firing a subordinate until everyone in the office is wondering why they haven't taken the step already.

Preparing the Grounds for the Divorce

Documentation of the troublesome employee's performance is critically important. Of course, you must keep such records for all your employees. If your company has a formal performance appraisal system, then you may be adequately covered.

Records are important because being sued for dismissing an employee is becoming more common. You should ask yourself, "If I have to, can I fully justify this dismissal?" If you can answer yes, that's all you need worry about.

Many supervisors agonize over every situation where they've had to let someone go. I prefer that a supervisor care too much than be completely callous about it.

Most of the firing situations don't develop overnight. Perhaps I've been extremely fortunate in my managerial life, but I've never had to fire anyone for getting into a fight and smacking someone in the mouth. That kind of situation, along with committing an office crime like stealing, clearly doesn't lend itself to my concept of "no surprise firings." Such situations are no doubt covered by company policy.

The more typical kinds of discharge that you're likely to run into in your managerial career have to do with poor performance and the employee's inability or unwillingness to abide by the company's standards. Some people will never be able to cut the job. They may get to a satisfactory training performance level but will never advance beyond that point to the performance level the job requires.

Firing is not the first thought that should come into your head. You must first satisfy yourself that the training has been correct and clearly understood. Was there any kind of personality barrier between the trainer and the trainee that impeded the flow of adequate information? Go back over the employee's aptitude tests, job application, and other initial hiring data on the chance that you may have missed something. Only after you're completely convinced that you have a below-satisfactory performer with little or no hope of bringing the performance up to proper standards should you consider termination as a possible solution.

Has the new employee been told that his or her performance is not up to the standard that is expected? You owe it to your people to let them know what the situation is. And that includes telling them when they're performing well. Too many managers assume that if employees don't get bad performance reports, they know they're doing okay. I've got news for you. Those employees believe you "don't give a damn"—and I think they're right on target.

Mergers and Buy-Outs

Since the mid-1970s, we have been seeing an onslaught of mergers and buy-outs. Usually, everyone is told that the new corporation is planning on no personnel changes, but within six months the personnel changes begin. A reorganization takes place and some people are fired. After a corporate take-over, everyone is scrambling to protect his or her own position. Some people survive and some don't. Those who do not survive are not necessarily inadequate. They may be filling positions that are duplicated in the parent organization. Some people are fired because they are too high in the organization or because their salary is too high.

If you get involved in one of these takeovers, you can only hope that the parent corporation is humane. If it is necessary to let some people go, it should be done in a way that acknowledges responsibility to these human beings. Continuing their salary for a reasonable length of time, providing office space and secretarial help while they look for a new position, and personal counseling are some methods used to soften the blow.

It is doubtful that you as manager will have anything new to tell employees about the takeover. You may get saddled with the job of telling some people in your area that they are being let go. It may even be possible that you have to select the people who are to be let go. You may have been told to reduce staff by 10 percent or reduce salary costs by 20 percent. These are difficult decisions because they often have little to do with performance. All you can do is carry out the task in as humane a manner as possible. Everyone knows the staff reduction is a result of the merger, so you might as well tie it to that; it at least allows people to save face. If they can't save their job, saving face is some consolation. Use whatever influence you have with the organization to generate some help for these people.

I have never been a great believer in seniority—countless

sins are committed in the name of "time in grade"—but if the last people hired are the first fired, at least none of them can complain that such a system is personal.

Downsizing

There's a relatively new business word in the last couple of decades: *downsizing*. As far as personnel are concerned, it's a synonym for reducing staff. *Downsizing* is a word that strikes fear in employee groups. We won't get into all the controversy of downsizing, except to say that it does not always achieve the desired results. We'll discuss two basic elements: your survival as an employee and the role you might be required to play as a new manager.

Your boss is going to be worried about her own survival, and she's going to be looking at your area of responsibility. The downsizing tremor is felt through the entire organization. Many managers and executives who thought they were immune from the "downsizing virus" end up being totally shocked.

The best advice I can give you is, "Don't let them see you sweat." Have confidence in your ability. Instead of going into your boss's office and trying to find out what your prospects are for survival, take a different approach. Asking about your survival is just another problem piled on your manager. Why not say, "I know that this is going to be a difficult time for you. I want you to know that I'm here to help you any way I can."

No one can guarantee your survival in a downsizing operation, but I suggest that you may increase the odds if you are a part of the solution rather than whining about your own job and putting an additional burden on your manager's shoulders.

As a manager, you may end up giving some bad news to people who are losing their jobs. The comments I made under mergers and buy-outs also apply to this section as a humane way to handle these personal contacts.

Let's hope that the organization you are a part of is a humane one that provides some help to people who are losing their jobs, with such items as salary continuance, continuation of health coverage for a reasonable length of time, and major assistance in helping find another job.

Even if you survive the downsizing, it's difficult to feel great about your good fortune when many of your friends did not fare as well. You may even feel a bit guilty about your survival, and that's a perfectly natural reaction for a humane manager.

A Second Chance

When an employee's job performance is unsatisfactory, it is important to make clear in your discussion with the employee that you're addressing yourself to the work and not to the person. At some point in the conversation you let the employee know that termination will come if the performance standards cannot be met. But it's not enough to let it go at that. Set a target for the employee to reach, in terms of both work improvement and time to achieve the goal. You have to be specific: "The average daily errors on this desk are ten. We need to cut that down to three errors per day by the end of the week." Your precise specifications serve a dual purpose. If the employee meets the goal, you may be on the way to solving the problem *and* retaining the employee. Failing that, you're ready to start the termination process.

Is it possible that this employee could handle some other job in your own area that is currently available? Or if an opening is coming up in accounting, can the employee make a contribution? Is this a situation where a person has been hired for the wrong job? Does the company gain anything by firing someone who might be useful somewhere else? Will the employee be so embarrassed by what appears to be failure that the stigma will carry over into future jobs? Is your company large enough that the employee could be moved to another area with no stigma? Former employees are part of a company's public. Can you handle the situation in such a way that you don't deplete your company's storehouse of civic goodwill? Even though the employee won't like being fired, can you handle the procedure so that the employee will admit to having been given every opportunity and will consequently agree that you had no choice in the matter?

Right here let me warn against taking the coward's way out and blaming the mysterious *they*. "As far as I'm concerned, ten errors a day isn't too bad, but *they* say we have to get it down to three, or *they* will force me to let you go." That indicates you're merely a puppet. Someone else is pulling the strings. You don't have a mind of your own.

You have to level with the employee who is not measuring up. I know of managers who sugarcoat all bad news to such an extent that the employee on the receiving end feels complimented on having done a clearly outstanding job.

Flexibility and Consistency

Some of your people will also need to be dismissed because of poor attendance. Companies have such a wide variety of sick-leave programs, however, that it's impossible to discuss what level of absenteeism is satisfactory. I personally don't care for sick-leave programs that allow, for example, one sick day per month or twelve per year, cumulatively. I prefer a method that allows supervisory discretion based on the individual situation. For example, I can decide not to dock a good, loyal employee for a day's absence. I can also decide that an employee with a bad attendance record has abused the privilege and must consequently be docked for a day's absence.

Admittedly, this kind of program is more difficult to administer than one with hard-and-fast rules to follow. In evaluating the merits of each case, you have to be able to defend your decision.

One disadvantage in having no formal program is the serious risk that decisions will not be made consistently throughout the company. Generous executives may be inclined to excuse almost any absence and pay the absentee; other managers may be more strict and dock for days missed. Having no formal program means the communication between departments and executives has to be extremely good, ensuring that approximately the same standards apply throughout the company.

The Dismissal Drama

So far we've discussed events leading up to a dismissal. Now let's talk about the dismissal itself. I'm referring to a dismissal whose timing you control.

My preference has always been to stage the drama on late Friday afternoon. By the time it's over, all the co-workers of the person being fired have left the office. Thus, the dismissed employee won't have to endure the humiliation of "clearing out" in front of an audience. Also, the employee can use the weekend to pull things together and prepare for seeking other employment, applying for unemployment compensation, or doing whatever else has to be done.

Any money due at the time of the dismissal should be given to the dismissed employee at the end of the interview. Being canned is enough of an emotional blow; wondering when the final check will arrive can only add to the misery. Severance pay—if that's the company's policy—should be given at the same time. Unused vacation time or sick leave should also be included in the compensation.

Put yourself in the other's position. You're not going to feel the termination was completely justified. Unless you receive every dollar you have coming to you, you'll probably think, "Well, I suppose I'll have to hire an attorney to get the money this chicken outfit owes me!" Remove that thought from the dismissed employee's mind by taking care of all those matters in advance.

Another courtesy that I think you owe the employee is to keep your intention to fire him or her as confidential as possible. Of course, the human resources and the payroll departments will have to know. But other than discussing it with the necessary management people, you should treat the matter confidentially.

The final scene in the dismissal drama is bound to be most uncomfortable for the supervisor. Because in that highly charged interview it's just the two of you face-to-face, and you want to get it over with as quickly as possible.

A good way to start is to review in brief what has happened. Don't drag it out and make it a recitation of all the other person's mistakes. I prefer something like this: "As you know from our past conversations, we had certain standards on the job that had to be met. I think we approached reaching those standards on a fair and reasonable basis. As I've mentioned to you from time to time over the past few weeks, the work is not up to those standards. I don't believe it's because of any lack of effort on your part. However, it hasn't worked out, and I don't think that comes as any surprise to you. We're going to have to terminate your services as of today. I really regret that. I wanted it to work out just as much as you did. But it hasn't worked out, and so we have to face up to reality. Here's the final check, including one month's severance pay plus your unused vacation and sick-leave time. This should give you a continuation of income for a time sufficient for you to find another job."

You can vary your remarks to fit the individual situation, but I think the above words say what needs to be said. They don't sugarcoat the bad news; I don't think they're too blunt either. You have to come up with a statement that fits the situation, and one you're comfortable with.

I assume there are no more companies that fire people by putting a pink slip in their pay envelope. That's inhumane, in my opinion. I can understand the necessity for it in a factory where thousands of people are all being temporarily laid off. I can also understand using the method if the entire business is being closed and everybody is going. Situations like that are not related to the performance of the individual. When someone is being let go because of a failure to perform or live up to company standards, the only way to handle it is on a one-on-one basis. The manager might prefer to avoid the direct confrontation, but it's part of the job's responsibilities and must be dealt with straight on.

When you consider it thoughtfully, you realize that keeping an unsatisfactory employee on the job is unfair not only to the company but also to the employee. No one is comfortable in a job he is not performing well.

I recall a situation a number of years ago where being canned turned out to be the biggest favor ever done for that young man. He was trying to function in an accounting position but was not cutting the mustard. After being let go, he decided to continue his education. He entered a law college and is now practicing his profession very successfully.

I find that people avoid the word *fire* as they do the word *die*. Instead of *die*, they say *pass away, go on to his reward,* or *cross over*. Instead of *fire*, they say *dismiss, discharge, let go, can.*

One last thought: You must be absolutely certain in your own mind that the firing is deserved. You must be sure you're being as objective as you can possibly be. If in doubt, use a more experienced executive as a sounding board. Then when you know you have to fire the employee, make sure it doesn't come as a surprise. And handle it in a considerate, humane, and delicate manner.

Three

The Manager as Administrator and Counselor

16

Secrets and Perceptions

Too many managers, both first-time and long-time, take some private pleasure in knowing something that others do not know. They assume that if you don't give others certain information, they don't know about it. That's an incorrect conclusion. If people don't know what's going on, they assume what is going on. What is worse, they may assume something that is not so, and even worse, they may act upon those incorrect assumptions.

You've probably heard this, and it's an important fact for managers to be constantly aware of. People don't act upon the facts; they act upon their perception of the facts. It is one of the manager's key duties to see that the facts and the perceptions are basically the same.

Very little that goes on in an organization needs to be secret. Oftentimes the things that are secret are merely a matter of timing: "We need to sit on this for a couple of weeks until the details are worked out."

The delight some managers feel in holding unnecessary secrets from staff is potential trouble, however. If people's assumptions about what was discussed at a managers' meeting are incorrect, and they act upon those false assumptions, you build your managerial career on a foundation of rotten timbers. It is more difficult to correct people's knowledge of what is *not so* than it is to let them know what *is so* in the first place.

A Typical Situation

In many organizations, there is a regularly scheduled managers' meeting—say, it takes place at 8:30 A.M. each Monday. This becomes known as the "Monday Morning Managers' Meeting." It's held every Monday except when a holiday is celebrated on Monday, in which case the meeting is held on Tuesday morning. (I've seen notices that have read "The Monday morning meeting will be held on Tuesday.")

If this is normally a one-hour meeting and you and a fellow manager come strolling back together, some of the staff will think or make comments like: "Well, I wonder what they decided today!" Or, "They've been gone three hours; something big is going on." Perhaps what really happened was that the local United Way executive had asked for a meeting to explain some organizational changes. Since your company is an important corporate citizen, the United Way is simply building corporate support. It doesn't directly affect the company, but it's a matter of community communication. The organization is holding a series of such informational meetings around town. The meeting about the United Way is fairly innocuous, but if you communicate nothing, some people are likely to assume that something big is going on.

Everyone has a need to know what is going on. In employee surveys, one of the higher rankings goes to, "a need to know of changes which affect me." People need to know even about things that may not affect them; if they know nothing, they assume something. Often that something is wrong and too often it isn't even close.

As a manager or executive, you are far better off in communicating too much than in communicating too little.

Let's assume that you have thirty people in your department and you have three section supervisors who are each responsible for ten people. The three section supervisors also have some work assignments of their own. (This arrangement is typical for the first step in management.) When you return from the Monday morning meeting, call the three supervisors into your office and give them a brief overview of what went on at the meeting. They can then inform their ten staffers. You cannot allow these supervisors to "keep it to themselves." They must communicate, too.

If you follow this approach consistently, you will build a staff who will say to friends in other departments, "Our manager does a good job of letting us know what is going on." If you do otherwise, you're going to have a lot of false information floating around to correct—if you ever know about it.

17

Your Relationship With the Human Resources Department

For years, I have avoided using the title "human resources" for the personnel function because I have not cared for the connotation. To me it sounds as though the company's personnel officers are in the mining business. The term appears to be here for a while—until some other buzz phrase comes along to replace it—so I must for now surrender to the inevitable.

The broadening of the title comes about, I suspect, because, as I explain later, in most organizations this department is also responsible for training and education, employee assistance programs, and administration of benefits, among many other functions. For purposes of this chapter, I'll use the initials HR, because that too has become commonplace.

A Manager's Involvement in Hiring

How much you will interact with HR will depend on how much latitude you're allowed in the selection process. In many companies, HR does the initial screening of prospective employees, but the final decision is left to the appropriate manager.

The overall selection process is strengthened if the final choice is made at the operating level. If a manager had nothing to say about the person hired and is unhappy with the choice, the new employee is the victim of a situation not of her doing. Fortunately, most companies do allow the operating department to make the final selection from several qualified candidates. The usual number is from three to five qualified candidates.

Sometimes new first-time managers are excluded from the hiring process by their own bosses. While this exclusion may be well intentioned, it is a serious mistake. The experienced manager should, at a very minimum, include the new manager in the process. And with some seasoning, he should allow that manager to select the people she will be held accountable for.

Managers have a far greater commitment to the success of selections they've made than they do for those who were selected for them and then assigned. The manager should not be able to think, "I never would have hired this idiot." There will be a temptation to think in those terms when the manager has been cut out of the process.

Although people working in HR consider themselves experts on selecting employees, it doesn't matter who they think is the best qualified if the person is someone you don't want. How you react to the recommendations of HR people is important. You must take their recommendations seriously. This assumes that through talks with you they fully understand what the job requires. If they don't, it's because you haven't given them the information they need. They can't be experts on every job in the company, even with access to all the job descriptions. You're the expert on the jobs in your area of responsibility, and you ought to know what's required.

Promotion and Other Employee Matters

You'll also become involved with the HR department in promotions. Most of the time you'll try to promote employees from your own area, but when you have to look to other areas of the company for the staff you need, the people in HR will be in a position to help you. For example, they can show you the original data collected when the person was hired, including scores from aptitude tests given at the time. In most cases, they'll consult with the department that employs your potential promotee and get important information you might not have gotten on your own.

Also, in some companies the HR department administers employee benefit programs, so you could be going to HR on behalf of subordinates who are having difficulties with some aspect of the program.

If you haven't managed people before, HR can be a strong resource for you. You can usually go there for advice and counsel on supervisory problems you've never encountered before. The HR department is also the usual repository for books on the management of people.

In many companies, the HR department handles the education and training of managers. Since this department serves the entire company, you can often talk with someone there about "people problems" that you might be reluctant to discuss with your own superior. So you can look to HR for assistance not only in selecting people but also in managing them.

I know of organizations that use the HR department as a place where employees can go with any problems they don't wish to discuss with their own boss. This can be a valuable service both to the employees and to the company. It is hoped that your HR department has been properly trained and educated in its function.

Not only will HR be able to assist you in your overall management but they can often be consulted about promotions up the managerial ladder. To be highly regarded in HR is a great asset, so don't be a stranger in their part of the building.

18

Personal and Organizational Loyalty

If there's one subject that has fallen into disrepute in recent years, it is loyalty. There's a prevailing attitude that loyalty should be withheld until it is clearly proven that it is deserved: The manager shouldn't receive loyalty until he or she has earned it. The employee shouldn't receive it until it is demonstrated it has been deserved. Lastly, the company doesn't receive loyalty until everyone—management and staff—feel it is justified. So in many organizations the lack of loyalty means less teamwork because no one trusts or is loyal to anyone else.

Loyalty Is Out of Fashion

Unfortunately, loyalty in business is not currently in vogue. Almost everyone feels that if one company acquires another, and the announcement is made that "we plan no personnel changes in the acquired company," it is a statement with no validity. The statement itself is perceived as the first step in a major reorganization and the subsequent loss of jobs. Such a perception is based on many examples of wholesale layoffs just a few months after reassurances to the contrary.

There have been many greedy, ruthless acts. There have also been some reorganizations and mergers that have been a matter of survival for the companies involved. People have witnessed friends in other companies being reorganized right out of their jobs. So we end up with some cynical boards, some greedy manipulators, and some concerned owners trying to save a company. At the same time, we see managers and employees who trust no one. What to do?

Showing loyalty is considered being a bit of a Pollyanna—or plain naïve. In many cases that may be fair, but if loyalty gets a bad rap, then it also follows that there may be times when it is withheld and it ought to be freely given.

Do we become cynical and never show loyalty? Or do we give our loyalty until it is proved that it is not deserved? There is much to recommend the second option. Being cynical not only hurts the organization, it hurts you personally. If you have a cynical, nontrusting attitude, you become a cynic. A comedian who is a cynic can be a brilliant performer. A manager who is a cynic is a tragedy.

So, it's in your best interest to be loyal, not only to the organization but also to your manager and your employees. This means not knocking your company in the community. It means not trashing the people you supervise. Even if there are times when you feel completely justified, avoid the temptation. Disparaging remarks say more about you than they do the object of your scorn. Give the organization and its people the benefit of the doubt. It's far better to assume that your loyalty is deserved than that it's not.

19

Job Descriptions, Performance Appraisals, and Salary Administration

Job descriptions, performance appraisals, and salary administration are valuable functions that every company performs, either formally or informally. But if the people administering them are not properly instructed in the purpose of these functions, they can be seriously mismanaged.

We have to speak of these functions from a conceptual viewpoint. Discussion of such precise details as the forms used is unfeasible because of the great variety in approaches that exist between industries and even between companies within individual industries.

Even companies without a formal program use such techniques—although often poorly. Informality is more likely to occur in smaller companies that are controlled by family members or by one or two people at the top. Such autocrats may feel they're being equitable and that all their employees are satisfied with the fair treatment they're receiving. That may indeed be the case, but the chances for it are remote. Even without a formal program, someone in charge decides which jobs are most important (job evaluation), makes a judgment on

how well people are doing (performance appraisal), and decides how much each employee is going to be paid (salary
administration). So even if the motto is "We're all like one
happy family, and as papa I make all the decisions on the basis
of what's fair," the company does have a program—with all
the idiosyncratic biases of the "papa" thrown in.

Job Descriptions

Most companies use job descriptions, although they may range
from very informal to highly structured descriptions. A job
description describes *what* is done in varying detail and it
usually includes hierarchical relationships.

Some companies write their own job descriptions; others
use a system designed by a management consulting service
whereby some company people are trained to write the descriptions and others are taught how to score the jobs to rank
them within the organization.

A job description typically tells what is done, the educational background required, how much experience is needed
to perform the work competently, what the specific accountability of the job is, and the extent of supervisory or management responsibility. The description may also spell out short-
term and long-term objectives and detail the relationships of
people involved, including what position each job reports to. It
will often mention the personal contacts the job requires, such
as with the public, either in person or by telephone. Consulting
services are giving greater recognition to the important relationships involved.

At some point, you'll write a job description, either for
yourself or for some of the people reporting to you. Some
companies allow the description to be written by the employee
and then reviewed and corrected, if necessary, by the manager.
It is best if the description is a joint effort by the employee and
the supervisor so that there is agreement as to what the job
entails. This avoids disagreements down the road.

The scoring of the job is usually done by a committee
specifically trained for that purpose. We will not discuss how,

because that varies by companies. The points usually arrived at will determine a salary range for each job, and the range may go from new and inexperienced to a fully seasoned professional on the job. If the midpoint salary of a job is considered 100 percent, then the bottom of the range could be 75 percent or 80 percent of that and the maximum for the outstanding performance would be 120 to 125 percent of that midpoint.

Since everyone knows that the score determines salary range, the score becomes crucial in many people's minds. Therefore, there is a tendency for people to overwrite job descriptions in the hope of enhancing the salary range. Filling a job description with such boilerplate copy usually works to a disadvantage. I served on a job evaluation committee for a number of years. A description that was puffed up forced the committee to wade through the hyperbole to get to the facts. We knew exactly what the writer was doing, so the puffing up had the opposite effect. On the other hand, job descriptions that were lean and to the point aided the committee in doing its work. So, if you write a job description, avoid the temptation to load it up. The scoring committee will resent your doing it.

Performance Appraisals

Performance appraisals can be as informal as telling someone "You've done a nice job" or as elaborate as a full-scale written report, complete with a long follow-up interview with the employee.

Clearly, all of us like to know how we're doing. One employee will say, "Working in this office is like working in the dark." Another will say, "Old Fussbudget may be tough, but you always know where you stand." It's meant as a compliment.

A formal system of performance appraisal—for example, one or two planned contacts with the employee each year for the specific purpose of discussing "how you're doing"—is preferable to the informal method, which is often equivalent to doing nothing.

Some managers are convinced that they communicate

effectively with their employees and that these employees know exactly how they stand. An interview with the employees, however, will indicate that communication is one of the greatest needs they feel.

Too many executives still approach their supervisory role with the motto "If they don't hear anything, they know they're doing okay." That doesn't cut it. Top-echelon managers too often avoid discussing all performances except those that require emergency action. They feel that performance appraisals are necessary for the rank and file but members of the executive team are above such things. The rationale is that these officials are clearly in control of the situation and of themselves and don't need to be told how they're doing. Just the opposite is true. Members of the executive team often have an even greater need to be told how their performance is viewed by their superiors.

The Appraisal Form

A formal system should be designed in such a way that it considers as many elements of the job as possible. The manager should be forced to make some judgment about each of the important factors. This means, first of all, that the executive must be knowledgeable about the job and the performance. That's why the appraisal should be done at the level closest to the job being reviewed. A manager three levels above the position in question can't handle the judgments as well as the manager in daily contact with the employee being appraised. It can be reviewed by higher-level management, but the appraisal will be more accurate when done by someone in daily contact with the job.

Here are some items that appear on a typical performance appraisal form. There may be anywhere from three to ten degrees of performance efficiency for each category, the extremes being "unsatisfactory" on the one end and "outstanding" on the other.

Volumes or production levels
Thoroughness

Accuracy (may be identified as error rate)
Initiative/self-starting
Attitude
Ability to learn
Cooperation/ability to work with others
Attendance and punctuality

You can probably think of other factors applying to your own business that ought to be included. Some systems may use a numeric weighting for each of the factors, arriving at a final rating that will be given to the employee. The entire form becomes a part of the employee's personnel file. The ranking scheme might be something like this:

80 to 100 points:	Outstanding
60 to 80 points:	Commendable
50 to 60 points:	Satisfactory
40 to 50 points:	Needs improvement
Less than 40 points:	Unsatisfactory

The ranges can be narrower or broader if your system requires it. You'll note that in this example, 50 to 60 points generates a performance description of "Satisfactory." In some companies, this would be entitled "Average Performance." *Satisfactory* is the better word. Most people resent being called average—they consider it demeaning. I believe the words *satisfactory* and *needs improvement* are more useful than *average* and *below average.* There are millions of average people in this world, but I've never known a satisfactory employee who thought he or she was just average.

Let's make another point about performance appraisals. Some managers have a rating in their mind, and they work backward to get it. You're "horsing the system" if you do that. It's usually done because the manager doesn't want to tell an employee that he needs improvement. But when you delay a tough decision, you're setting yourself up for much greater problems down the road.

The Interview

The interview with the employee about the performance appraisal becomes crucial. You should plan to hold it at a time when you'll be unhurried and not likely to be interrupted. Allow yourself as much time as is needed to cover all facets of the job. Answer all questions. Listen to everything the employee wants to say. Your willingness to hear your subordinate out may be as important as the discussion itself. Employees are so used to dealing with managers who behave as though everything is an emergency that, when given time to talk to their superior about their own dreams and aspirations, they may feel uncomfortable.

The conversation with your subordinate is so important that you should instruct your secretary to hold your telephone calls. This should include even calls from the president of the company. Of course, anyone in any organization can be interrupted for emergencies, but you should not take phone calls of a routine nature. It's quite disconcerting to be telling another about your ambitions and feelings only to have the other break the spell by taking phone calls.

We're slaves to the telephone to an extent that's difficult to understand. How many times have you been outside the door and gone rushing back into the house to answer the phone only to find it's a magazine salesman? Somehow, there's an urgency about a telephone ringing that demands response.

Getting back to the performance appraisal interview, you should direct the tone of the discussion but not dominate it. You definitely have a message to convey. You want to go over each performance appraisal factor with your subordinate. You want to make known what you consider to be your subordinate's strengths on the job and what areas require some improvement. You'll seldom get disagreement on the areas you designate as strengths. But you're likely to encounter disagreement when you get around to discussing weaknesses. And this is where you have to allow employees to express their own feelings.

Some people will never hear anything positive if it follows something they consider negative, such as an area that "needs improvement." As a result, never start off a performance appraisal meeting with anything that might be construed by the staffer as negative. Start with a couple of positives.

Do you have documentation that indicates where the employee is weak and where improvement is needed? Your case is much stronger if buttressed by hard evidence. Production or quality records are much more convincing than an executive's intuition. When you come up against the subordinate's disagreement, that difference of opinion is important and should be discussed. It's possible that you're wrong, but you won't be if the facts can be documented.

An experiment I once engaged in was a great help to me in getting the staff to understand performance appraisals. Before sitting down to make my Solomon-like judgments, I gave all the members of my staff a blank form and asked them to evaluate their own performance. We then compared their appraisals with mine; with only one exception, their ratings were lower than mine. I'm not a liberal grader, so that wasn't the reason. We were then able to discuss our views of each factor rated. They learned a great deal about performance appraisal from the experiment, but I learned a great deal more about the people I was managing.

Too many leaders will be thorough in pointing out the areas in which the employee should show improvement, but they will not go far enough. If they're going to tell the employee where job performance is not up to expectations, then they must also tell *how* it can be improved. This needs to be thought through in great detail before the interview is even held.

The Agenda

This brings us to the preparation time that I believe is essential to a successful performance appraisal interview. You should sit down and decide what points you want to cover in the conversation. You might even prepare a brief outline of what you want to discuss. It's possible that the performance appraisal form your company uses may trigger all the proper thoughts in your mind. However, you must anticipate that it will not. You'll look quite foolish if you fail to cover all the bases and have to ask the employee to come back into your office a day later to review some important point that you forgot.

I recommend that you actually make an outline of the significant items you should cover. Here are some questions you might ask as you prepare the outline:

- What areas of this employee's performance or attitude should you mention?
- What areas not covered in the performance appraisal do you need to mention?
- What are some of the items of personal interest about this employee that you should bring up?
- What questions should you ask this employee that are likely to generate some conversation and opinions about the work?
- How can you help this employee do a better job? What are the areas in which this employee will be self-motivated?
- How can you let this employee know she is important to you personally, not just for the work performed?
- How does this employee fit into the company's future plans? Is this person promotable? What can you do to help?

I'm sure you get the idea of the kind of self-examination you should go through before beginning the session with the employee. A few minutes spent preparing for the conversation will greatly increase the success ratio of your performance appraisal interviews.

The Satisfactory Employee

Many executives prepare quite thoroughly for the interview with the problem employee. They know it might get sticky and they'd better see to it that their flanks are protected. You should be just as thorough in preparing for the interview with the satisfactory employee. Occasionally you'll be surprised by the outstanding staff member who'll turn a conversation you thought was going to be all "sweetness and light" into a real donnybrook.

As you spend more years in management, you'll find that the satisfactory employee generally uses this interview to unload some of the problems that have been festering. The problems vary with the situation. Here are some examples:

"I'm not advancing fast enough."

"My salary is not fair for the work I do."

"My co-workers are not performing up to standards."

"As manager, you don't pay enough attention to subordinates who are getting the job done."

"Good performance is not appreciated or recognized."

You should welcome such input from your satisfactory employees, even though you risk hearing what you don't want to hear. Let's face it, many employees will tell you only what they think you want to hear; but a rare and precious few will be truth-tellers, and these you must listen to carefully. Don't fall into the "shoot the messenger" syndrome. Although the news a messenger brings you makes you unhappy, the fault is not with the messenger; punishing the carrier won't change the truth of the message carried. Ignorance may be bliss, but it can be fatal in a managerial career.

Of course, the information you're receiving may not exactly reflect the facts. But even though you're receiving it through the carrier's filters, that doesn't make it any less valuable. You've been around long enough to know how to sort out what's important and what's window dressing. If the satisfactory employee believes it's important enough to bring to your attention, then you ought to listen to it. Besides, this subordinate surely knows you prefer a trouble-free interview to one filled with problems, so you know the matter would not have come up unless the employee felt strongly about it.

It's possible that you may occasionally have a mischief maker on your hands, but such people are usually not your highly satisfactory employees.

An Open-Door Policy

"My door is always open." How many times have you said it
yourself? It doesn't take the employees long to find out what
the statement really means.

"My door is always open, as long as you don't come in
here to tell me about any new problems." That's one possible
meaning. "My door is always open, but don't come in to talk
about money or a better job." That's another. "My door is
always open, but I don't want to hear about your personal
problems." Your employees know what you really mean or
they soon figure it out.

These same supervisors are likely to also say, or think, "I
don't want my people to like me. I just want them to respect
me." Don't you find it easier to respect people you like?

Your performance appraisal interviews should encourage
your subordinates to say whatever they have in mind. The
more open the communication between you, the better chance
that you'll have a satisfactory working relationship.

Salary Administration

It should be pretty obvious that job descriptions, performance
appraisals, and salary administration all fit together in one
overall plan. They're designed to provide accurate descriptions
of what people do, give fair evaluations of their performance,
and pay them a salary that's reasonable for their effort. All
these factors must bear a proper relationship to one another
and make a contribution to the organization's overall goals.

If you have a job evaluation program, you probably also
have salary ranges for each position in the organization. As a
manager, you work within that scale.

It makes sense to have a minimum and a maximum salary
for each position. You can't allow a situation to develop in
which an individual could stay on the same job for years and
receive a salary out of all proportion to what the task is worth.
It's important to make certain that long-term employees are
aware of this situation, especially as they get close to the salary

"lid" on the job. For most well-qualified people this is not a problem, because they'll usually be promoted to another job with a larger salary range. However, in your managerial career you will encounter long-term employees who remain in the same jobs. Perhaps they don't want to be promoted. Perhaps they are at their level of competence and cannot handle the next position up the ladder.

These people need to know that there is a limit to what the job is worth to the organization. You have to tell these individuals that once they are at the maximum, the only way they can receive more money is if the salary ranges are changed on all jobs. This may happen, for example, through a cost-of-living increase that raises the ranges on all jobs by a certain percent. Should that occur, you will have a little room for awarding salary increases.

Nonetheless, long-term employees who stay in the same job for an extended period of time and who are at maximum salary level need to have continued incentive. They are capable and should be kept on the job. Many companies have solved this problem by instituting annual financial awards (such as annual, increasing cash stipends) related to years of service. This keeps financial payments out of the job evaluation system and yet rewards the faithful long-term employee.

The salary administration program for all other employees usually includes a salary recommendation within a range of pay increases, based on the kind of performance appraisal the employee has received. Since the two procedures have such an impact on each other, some companies separate the salary recommendation from the performance appraisal rating. In that way a supervisor's idea of what a salary increase ought to be is not allowed to determine the performance appraisal given. If as supervisor you make both determinations at the same time, you'll be tempted to take the answer you want and work backward to justify it. It remains difficult to separate salary consideration from the performance appraisal, but completing the procedures several weeks or months apart may help.

So let's assume your company does have salary ranges for each job and there's some limitation on what you can recommend. No doubt the salary ranges overlap. For example, a veteran employee on a lower-level job could be paid more than a newer employee on a higher-level job. Or an outstanding performer at one level could be paid more than a mediocre worker one level up.

Equity

As the manager, you're concerned with equity. You should review the salaries of all the people who report to you. You might begin by listing all the jobs in your department, from top to bottom. You might then write the monthly salary next to each name. Based on what you know about the job performances, do the salaries look reasonable? Is there any salary that looks out of line?

Another method you can use is to rank the jobs in the order of importance to the department, as you perceive the situation. How does that compare with top management's evaluation of the importance of the jobs? If there are differences you can't reconcile or accept, then you'd better schedule a session with your immediate superior to see what can be done about it.

In this matter of rankings, appraisals, and salaries, a word of caution is in order. Recognize, and be willing to admit to yourself, that you like some employees more than others. You're conning yourself if you think you like them all equally. Certain personality types are more agreeable to you than others. Try as honestly as you can to keep these personality preferences from unduly influencing the decisions you make about appraisals, salaries, and promotions.

In recommending salary increases for several subordinates, you'll have some tricky decisions to make. If the company makes all its salary adjustments at the same time each year, then it's fairly easy to compare one recommendation against another. You can make all your decisions at one time and see how they stack up with one another. But if salary decisions occur throughout the year—for example, if they are tied to the worker's employment anniversary—it's more difficult to have all the decisions spread out in front of you.

Although maintaining equity in this type of situation is

difficult, it is possible if you keep adequate records. Retain copies of all your job descriptions, performance appraisals, and salary recommendations. Some companies encourage supervisors not to keep such records and to depend on the personnel department's records. I believe that maintaining your own set is worth the effort; you'll then have the records when you want them. Keep such records in a file that is locked, and do not allow any employee access to the file, including the secretary or assistant who works closely with you.

The Salary Recommendation

In making a salary recommendation, be as sure as you possibly can that it's a reasonable amount. It should be neither too low nor too high and at the same time fit within the framework of the performance the company is receiving from that person. An increase that's too high, for example, could create an "encore" problem. Anything less than the same amount offered the next time around may be considered an insult by the employee. However, an unusually large increase coming at the time of a promotion doesn't run that same encore danger because it can be tied to a specific, nonrepeating situation. In that case, you must explain to the employee why the increase is so large and why it doesn't create a precedent for future increases.

Since a small increase can be considered an insult, you'd perhaps do better to recommend no increase at all rather than a pittance. Sometimes a small increase is a cop-out and is given because the supervisor lacks the courage to recommend no increase. But this only postpones the inevitable reckoning; I recommend confronting the situation immediately and honestly.

When considering the amount of the raise, it's essential that you not allow the employee's need to be an important factor. Before you think I'm being inhumane, consider these points. If you based salary increases on need, the employee in the most desperate state of need would be the highest paid. If that person were also the best performer, you'd have no problem. But what if the employee's performance was merely average?

The common thread that must run through salary administration is merit. Basing your salary recommendations on who has been with the company the longest, who has the greatest number of children, or whose mother is ill moves you away from your responsibilities as a salary administrator and puts you in the charity business. If you have subordinates with financial problems, you can be helpful as a friend, a good listener, or a source of information about where to go for professional assistance, but you can't use the salary dollars you're charged with as a method of solving the social problems of your subordinates.

When you're making a salary adjustment for a subordinate who's having difficulty, there's a great temptation to add a few more dollars than you would otherwise. You must resist that temptation and base your decision strictly on the performance of the individual employee.

20

It May Not Be the Money

I was involved in the daily management of people for many years, yet there was one situation that no one ever told me about. I had to discover it on my own. When I finally did figure it out, it was a revelation. I call it one of those "aha" experiences. Once it occurs to you, you chastise yourself for not having realized it before. It could fit in many chapters in this book, but because of its unique properties, I have decided to assign it a brief chapter of its own.

The Real Source of Discontent

Every once in a while, an employee would start talking to me about a need for more money. Sometimes it would be one of the better staffers, and the encounter would come as a big surprise to me because I knew of no problem with this employee.

The employee might even be a longtime associate who knew very well that salary increases were allocated only once a year, on the anniversary of the employee's starting date.

I finally figured out that when an employee comes in to ask for a raise, *the real issue may not be the money*. It may be a situation that she is converting into a money problem. The person may not even be aware of the link. If the employee is unhappy about a situation, she thinks, "I am not being paid enough to put up with this." The employee and the manager now talk about money, but they are not getting at the root cause of the discontent because the manager is hearing only what's being said.

One reason I didn't stumble upon this sooner is that it happens infrequently. But after I made the connection, my entire approach changed. I would invite the employee to sit down and converse about how things were going. By asking questions, listening, and not appearing to be rushed, I would eventually tap into the real area of discontent, and we could start dealing with the actual problem.

Occasionally, it would in fact be the money, but even then the request came out of the blue and was often triggered by a specific event, such as, "My son's car is about to be repossessed. He's missed four payments."

Oftentimes—in fact, more often than not—if you could magically make the money appear, the underlying problem would still remain. In the case of the car payments, the son's fiscal irresponsibility isn't resolved by granting the parent an increase in salary that has nothing to do with performance.

Other times, you may find that a strained relationship with a co-worker is the basis of the problem. You know by now, through life experience, that the problems humans encounter are as varied as pebbles on the beach. In management, never be surprised about what surprises you.

So the next time someone walks into your office and says, "I have to have more money," you now have another arrow in your quiver.

21

Is There Such a Thing as Motivation?

For too many managers, this is their definition of motivation: To get you to do what I want you to do, with a minimum of trouble from you. That's authority, pure and simple.

At one time a psychological consulting firm was working in our office. During a feedback session the psychologist assigned to me commented that I was reluctant to use the power of my position to get things done and that I was more interested in persuading people. He meant it as constructive criticism, but I accepted it as a compliment and still do.

I believe one of the greatest strengths of a leader is the ability to get the job done without having to reach back and use the power of the position. I know it's there. I can always reach back and use it if I have to. But isn't the power of the position just as strong if I don't use it? Doesn't my use of the power mean I'm desperate, unable to achieve my objectives in any other way? Clearly, it's more of a resource when I don't use it.

Self-Motivation

The only motivation that really works is self-motivation. When you do a job because you want to, your motivation is self-perpetuating. You don't have to be bludgeoned into doing it.

One of the primary responsibilities of a manager is to change the feelings of subordinates from "have to" to "want to."

Also, a good manager gets the job done by finding out how different people respond. If they're self-motivated, they're self-motivated either to get the job done or to just get by. They react in different ways, and you need to understand them well enough to know how they react and to what.

Some people are self-motivated by the possibility of a promotion. As soon as they see a relationship between their current performance and a promotion, they'll strive to perform at the top of their efficiency. Others seek their manager's approval. Since satisfactory performance is how they receive the approval, that's the route they follow. Still others like to compete in a friendly way with their peers. They want to be the best performer in the area and so will work hard at achieving that objective.

Many people are working simply for the dollar, and the way to get more dollars is to perform well to maximize the next salary increase. Many others take great personal pride in doing whatever they do well. Depending on the condition of the labor market, a number of people will be working hard to keep from being unemployed.

Some workers bring their feeling for family into their attitude toward the job, but that's often tied in turn to one of the other reasons I've mentioned—pursuing the dollar. They want to be able to provide more for the family, which requires more dollars.

The Manager's Role

Learning how to maximize the performance of staff is a permanent part of your daily work life. You'll have varying levels of turnover, and turnover brings in new people. You need to get to know and understand them. Your obligation in this matter deserves particular emphasis. Employees want to be understood. They want to feel important as people, not as pieces of production to get the job done. Your genuine concern for them will shine through in all you do. To understand and appreciate them doesn't mean you need be a parent figure. And you need not compromise your principles as far as quality of work is concerned.

Concern for and understanding of your staff are signs of management strength, not weakness. The so-called tough, autocratic boss may achieve satisfactory results for a while, but over the long haul the destroyer inevitably becomes the destroyed.

Too many managers believe that if you're fair, concerned, and understanding, you can't be tough when the situation demands or requires it. Nothing is further from the truth. It actually makes the show of authority much more effective because it is so rarely displayed.

Here's an area that you have to handle with skill and diplomacy. You'll recall we previously mentioned that some of your staff may be self-motivated because of what they can do for their families. Some employees will respond very favorably to your interest in their families. There are others who will consider personal inquiries an invasion of their privacy. So how to handle these contradictory positions? If an employee on his own offers information about his family, you can then inquire about the family. In conversation, you'll learn about spouse, children, hobbies, and other interests. With such an employee, you can make an inquiry such as, "How did Jeff and his team do in Little League last night?" This is a prime example of getting to know your employees, with their permission, and it fits right into the concept that everyone is not motivated by the same things.

If you have an employee who never volunteers anything about his personal life, leave it alone and don't violate the obvious desire for privacy.

Shortly after I was moved into management, I was "nickled and dimed to death" by employees selling Scout cookies, candy bars, raffle tickets, and other worthwhile projects limited only by the imagination. Eventually, I set aside a dollar amount in the family budget each month. I would buy one of any product being offered that was modestly priced. In other words, I'd buy one box of Scout cookies instantly, but I would turn down a $10 raffle ticket on a golf cart for the local church bazaar.

Once a dad who was trying too hard to make his daughter's quota pressed me to buy two boxes of cookies. My reaction was, "Do you realize how much of this stuff I carry home?" It's okay to be accommodating, but quite another to be taken advantage of.

Of course I was an easy mark for everyone who reported to me, but I could say no very easily to people from other departments who solicited me. "No thanks. I buy all these goodies from the folks in our department." The few extra dollars that this cost me each year was worth it for the good public relations with the staff.

Assuming you had only one parent selling cookies, you could even say, "Mary, isn't it about time for the cookie drive? Tell Kim to save a box for me." People reporting to you will appreciate that kind of attitude because most co-workers hate to see them coming with cookies in hand.

In getting to know your employees, there is a tendency to work with the new people and ignore the seasoned employees who do an outstanding job. Of course, it's important to bring the new people up to speed, but you must never take the outstanding employees for granted. The outstanding achievers need to know how much their quality performance is noticed and appreciated.

The Role Played by Titles

The value of titles is underestimated in too many organizations.

Titles don't cost a company anything, so you ought to be liberal in using them as long as you maintain equity within the organization. For example, you can't have one department quite liberal in the use of titles and another very conservative.

The banking industry is well known for this practice, and although some executives in other businesses put them down for it, I think the banks know exactly what they're doing. A customer of a bank dealing with the Vice President—Consumer Loans will feel much more gratified than if dealing with a loan clerk. The spouse of the Vice President—Consumer Loans is surely a greater booster of the bank than the spouse of the loan clerk. In every possible way, the bank's standing in the community is elevated by this liberality with its titles.

The strange thing is that the vice president in this instance may have the same duties as the loan clerk. But which one has the more positive self-image and the stronger self-motivation? The answer is obvious.

As you move up the corporate ladder, you may have an opportunity to influence your company's policy in the use of titles. There must be an orderly manner in their use. You don't start a new employee with a super title for a routine clerical position. The title is there for the employee to aspire to.

A company's morale can be increased dramatically by a more enlightened use of titles. Titles can go a long way toward giving an employee a sense of well-being and of being appreciated. Once during a salary freeze, I sensed that the secretary reporting to me was motivated by title and position. I said, "If you have no objection, I'm going to change your title from *secretary* to *staff assistant*." The reaction far exceeded any positive response from previous salary increases.

We all want to feel important, and so do our employees. Let's help them experience that feeling.

The Status Symbol

Another matter that falls in the motivation area is the status symbol. Obviously, status symbols work or they wouldn't find so widespread an application in the business world.

The key to the executive washroom has almost become a joke. I don't understand how anybody can be turned on about this, but perhaps I don't understand the washroom psychology. The size of the office, the luxuriousness of the carpeting, wooden versus steel furniture, executive parking privileges, an executive dining room, company-paid club memberships, company-leased automobiles for executive use, corporate aircraft—the proliferation of status symbols is limited only by the expansiveness of the human imagination.

All could be considered as attempts to inspire people to raise their aspirations. These things are not important in themselves, but indicate that the employee is recognized as having arrived at a certain level in the organization. They're a lot more important to those who don't have them than to those who do. As a friend of mine says about money, "Why is it that most of the people who say money isn't important are just the ones who have plenty of it?" The same goes for status symbols.

A company should not become overly concerned about status symbols, but if it makes them available to its employees, it should not then criticize those same employees for longing after these "methods of keeping score." Actually, for most people, it's not the acquisition of the symbols that's important; it's what they signify to other people. Most status symbols would fall by the wayside if no one else knew you had achieved them.

It's fine to want to attain certain status symbols, but it's important that you keep them in proper perspective. Don't let them become so critical to you that it'll tear you up if you don't attain them as quickly as you think you should.

You cannot substitute status symbols for a satisfactory salary program or a good management approach. Unfortunately, some managers and even some companies think otherwise. They treat people badly or pay them below the competition and then figure they can make up for it with status symbols. Such an attitude is an insult to the intelligence of the subordinate. If the subordinate buys it, the insult is deserved.

Status symbols are the icing on the cake; they are not the cake itself. When used with intelligence and some insight into human behavior, they can be a valuable tool—but a tool is no better than the person using it.

22

The Generation Gap

First-time managers can be, and are, all ages. In my management seminars, I have all ages of new or prospective managers. Although most are in their twenties, thirties, and forties, a few are in their fifties and sixties.

Three situations exist with regard to age differences between managers and the people reporting to them: (1) the mature manager supervises people who are younger; (2) the young manager supervises people who are older; and (3) the mature or young manager leads a group of varied ages, some younger, some older, and some of the same generation.

The greatest conflicts seem to occur when a young manager supervises older workers. For some reason, mature people seem to resent working for a young manager. The line most often used—and used to the point of being a cliché—is that the young manager is not "dry behind the ears." A large part of this problem is the attitude of the older employee, exacerbated by the impetuousness of youth. The situation must be dealt with. Therefore, we will deal primarily with the problems encountered by a young manager supervising a workforce predominately older than herself.

Your approach should be nice and easy. You want the staff to think of you as mature beyond your years. If everything you do creates that impression, sooner or later it becomes a fact in everyone's mind.

Take time making changes; go slow. Don't throw your weight around by making decisions right and left, and too quickly. Many older employees will read quick decisions as being impulsive (even though they might not think the same thing if done by an older supervisor). Quick action by an older manager gives him the adjective "decisive." The same action by a young manager earns him the adjective "impetuous." It's not fair, but that's the way it is. What you need to do is give people time to get used to your being there. So don't build any barriers that you later have to dismantle.

Mistakes to Avoid

Often, the new manager makes changes right away, avoids the rule of incremental change, and uses all the newfound authority. That approach upsets everyone, but is especially irritable to employees who have been around a while.

You don't have to know the answer to every question brought to you. Faking an answer when you don't know it is a mistake, and the experienced employee sees through it instantly. If you can't answer a question say, "I don't know, but I'll find out and get back to you." This candor avoids the image of the know-it-all kid. In the minds of many older employees, and many not so old, you haven't lived long enough to have all the answers.

Demonstrate early on and often that, like all good managers, you are concerned about the well-being of every person reporting to you. As a manager, you need to be a salesperson. Your job is to sell your employees on the concept that they are all fortunate to have you.

Strategies for the Young Manager

Make your older employees more comfortable with your supervision by delaying some of the commonsense and fairly obvious decisions you have to make as manager. *You* know that you can make them almost immediately, but when you are new on a job, occasionally postpone your decision when it will do no damage to show your reflection on the matter. For example, if an older employee brings you a problem that he considers serious, but about which you feel you can make an immediate decision, consider saying, "Let me think about that for a while and I'll get back to you tomorrow morning." That way you indicate that you are thoughtful and want to get all the facts, thus dispelling the young, know-it-all image. You also show that you are *not* impetuous, which is a frequent complaint about young managers. That's an interesting "two-fer."

Or, in the same situation, you might consider (with emphasis on the word *consider*) asking, "Do you have a recommendation?" or "What do you think ought to be done?" If the person bringing the problem strikes you as having common sense, give it a try. But if he's someone who builds you a clock when you ask the time, you may be better off passing on this idea.

There is some advantage in reviewing the past performance appraisals of your subordinates when you take on a managerial job, but remember to keep an open mind. The appraisals may be generally correct, but we've all known managers with blind spots about certain staff members. I once inherited an employee who supposedly never had an original idea, but by using a different approach I was able to receive some good ideas from her. So don't give up on people too soon; you may find you have the ability to reach them.

Finally, unless you already know your new, older subordinates personally, consider using last names only until they suggest otherwise. Many mature folks consider younger people too familiar or presumptuous. Of course, if you are being promoted from within an office where everyone uses first names, stick to the norm. However, if you're coming in from outside, try the Mrs. Jones or Mr. Smith approach until you're fully accepted.

23

Helping to Prepare for the Gold Watch

Although helping people prepare for retirement is a company-wide responsibility, your involvement as their supervisor is crucial because to a large extent you represent the company to prospective retirees. You're involved in managing their day-to-day activities and you therefore have the greatest contact with them.

The thought may occur to you that it's a bit odd to be talking about retirement in a book that is aimed at the new manager. It would indeed be odd if we were talking about your own retirement, but since it could happen at any time to someone under your supervision, you must be prepared for it.

I would even suggest that you become acquainted with prospective retirees in your area as soon as you assume your new duties. You'll have to administer the company's program for them. Some companies don't have such a program. In that case your role becomes even more significant.

Many organizations provide graduated time off over the last few working years to help the employee get used to the idea of not coming into the office. This may create some work scheduling problems for you as a manager. You can't replace the prospective retiree prematurely because you want that person to feel needed right up to the day of departure. On the other hand, you can't completely ignore the staffing problems created by the employee's more frequent absences. Some kind of temporary arrangement is best, even if it means using some part-time help. You should not expect your existing staff to pick up the slack unless it can be conveniently handled through duty reassignments.

I know of one situation where a retiring employee—a woman—was told by her male supervisor that she could have virtually unlimited vacation time during her last year on the job. All she had to do was let the supervisor know well in advance when she was going to be gone. This was done. But because he hadn't planned for it, the supervisor had a workload problem. He reacted by getting miffed at the retiring employee every time she talked about exercising the company policy and taking time off. As a result, she stopped taking the time off. He solved his staffing problem, but he failed as an executive in his responsibility to help this woman prepare for her retirement in the way she had wanted to. That's a rotten solution to a staffing problem. In addition, that employee's recollection of the company is colored by the last year on the job, during which she could not avail herself of what was a stated company policy.

The Company Program

Many companies prepare their employees for retirement through an official company program that's usually administered by the personnel department. In addition to time off, such a program may include individual counseling, discussion of Social Security and Medicare benefits, hobby and craft demonstrations, exploration of the availability of community programs with members of those agencies invited to lead discussions and to answer questions, seminars with trained professionals about the psychology of preparing for retirement, discussions on budget preparation and adjustment to retirement, information about income tax implications for retired people with individual consultation, and any other service that a company may consider appropriate for helping people prepare for this major change in their lifestyle.

If your company does have such a program, you're part of

an enlightened organization, and your involvement in the process will be primarily supportive. But if your company has no program, or one that isn't very comprehensive, then your own involvement should become heavier.

However, you shouldn't have much of a problem. Many people who are getting close to retirement look forward to it as the opportunity to do things they haven't had time to do thus far in their lives—and they usually do a good job of preparing themselves for it. Your involvement with them will not be difficult. It will again be primarily a supportive role.

Mandatory and Voluntary Retirement

Except for certain exempt occupations such as airline piloting, law enforcement, and the military, legislation now prohibits mandatory retirement. An individual can work as long as he wants, and stays productive.

The employee who doesn't want to retire and who dreads that terrible day is tough to work with. Such people, if they are no longer productive, often see themselves as being rewarded for thirty years of faithful service by being "put out to pasture." Work is their life. You can help such people by listening to them and making suggestions as to where they might find part-time work after retirement. The most valuable service you can provide is your sympathetic attention so that they can talk about their feelings as they try to adjust to the inevitable.

Before mandatory retirement at a given age was forbidden by law, there was much controversy about the concept. Frankly, there were valid arguments on both sides of the question. The fact that the law was changed does not destroy the validity of the issues, and people working in management still have to deal with them.

If everyone were required to retire at a specified age, everyone would be treated the same. Knowing when someone was going to retire would give younger people in the organization some knowledge about when certain promotional opportunities would occur. That way, training and development could be planned on an orderly basis. In addition, judgments about the continued competency of those who work to more advanced ages would not have to be made.

Another advantage of everyone's retiring at the same age is that "the system" determines when people retire; it isn't management deciding when someone has to hang it up because they are no longer as productive as the job requires. This situation gets sticky when the employee believes that the quality and the quantity of her performance are still satisfactory but when management and the facts indicate otherwise.

One strong argument against any mandatory retirement age is that individuals with valuable experience are lost to the company. Many older workers are alert, in satisfactory health, and able to work for additional years. Retirement, the argument goes, should be based on competency. People who are able to get the job done should be allowed to work as long as they can produce.

However, the removal of a mandatory retirement age creates the potential for bitter feelings and resentment. Employees who want to continue working, but are told to retire because of deteriorating performance, feel as though they are being fired. That is not the way to end a long and distinguished career. Nevertheless, the employee who continues to work indefinitely must recognize the potential for this kind of ending. I'm reminded of outstanding entertainers who cannot give up when they are at their peak. As their powers diminish, they become pathetic figures, still looking for adulation and applause. The few who remain at the top are rare. How much better to go while the audience is still clamoring for just one more.

Your Own Role

As the employee gets closer to retirement, you should indicate that you're available for consultations about the event. You show your interest by calling the employee into your office and asking how his retirement plans are coming along. Some executives tell employees, "You know my door is always open. If you're having any problems, be sure to come in." Most employees will not respond to that kind of invitation. Rather, they'll view it as a polite brushoff. Unless they have a serious problem to talk over with you, there's a good chance they won't come in.

You must take the initiative. Don't wait for prospective retirees to come in on their own. Most of them will not want to bother you with what they might consider chit-chat. They may think you're too busy for them even though you are not. You're never too busy for your people.

Periodically, call such an employee into your office. If you have the facilities, share a cup of coffee. You can start off with such a simple question as "How is your planning for retirement coming along?" If that doesn't get the conversation going, keep probing until you find a subject that does generate some interest. If you know the employee well, you will know the keys to initiating a friendly conversation. If you don't, a few discreet inquiries in the department will provide some answers.

Here are several other questions that may get the employee to open up and start talking:

"How does your husband [wife] feel about your retirement?"

"Do you have any trips planned for your retirement?"

"Have you worked out your retirement budget as yet?"

"Do you plan on continuing to live in this area after you retire?"

"How do your children feel about your retirement? Do they have a positive attitude about it?"

"What one aspect of retirement do you think about the most?"

I'm sure you can think of many other questions that will help to initiate conversation.

The fact is that what may start out as a low-key, casual conversation may turn into a more serious discussion about the real concerns the prospective retiree has on his or her mind.

Many managers feel that the "out of sight, out of mind" approach is better. They incorrectly reason that they are asking for problems and that enough problems exist without seeking them out. The question is then whether they find out about the problems or not. Your interest in listening to your subordinates' plans for the future and learning about their misgivings as they move into the retirement phase of their life could be very helpful to them. Don't deny them that benefit.

Four
Preparing and Improving Yourself

24

The Role of Self-Discipline

While self-discipline is important in all aspects of life, it is essential in the role of a manager. You will find chapters in this book that will assist you in many areas where self-discipline is a vital factor.

Though it may be possible, I have never known a person who lacked self-discipline in his personal life yet who had a goodly supply of it on the job. I don't believe you turn self-discipline off and on like a hot water faucet.

A person who is well disciplined is not a procrastinator. There are not many situations that are improved by putting them off.

When mail arrives in the in-box, a self-disciplined person will dispose of as much of it as possible, right then. Why handle it twice (or more) if you don't have to? Instead, many people go entirely through the mail, and then stack it up with the idea that they will get back to it later. Of course, there may be items that you have to discuss with someone who may not be available right now. And we all know that much of the mail that comes across our desks can go directly to the wastebasket.

A system that I worked out for myself had me do the following as I went through the mail:

1. What could be tossed went immediately to the wastebasket. (Rarely did I ever retrieve it.)

2. For what needed to be referred to someone else on the staff, I made a handwritten note in the margin or at the top. "Sally: look over, recommend, and return. LB" It went into my out-box.
3. For those items I could dictate into the system, I dictated right then. ·
4. For those items that I needed to have a personal discussion with someone, I marked "Talk to Fred" and place it in my pending box. I tried to empty the box daily.
5. If the item was internal and I could, I responded with a speed memo and placed it in my out-box.

My basic rule was to never keep any paper in my office that I could dispose of.

I handled in-box mail once each day. Rush items were placed in the middle of my desk and items that I called "the sky is falling work" were placed on the seat of my chair.

There is a temptation for people to put off doing unpleasant tasks. But if you put them off, the prospect remains with you much longer. Why not tackle the tough job now and remove the lengthy prospect of the unpleasant task?

Diplomacy and Self-Discipline

A self-disciplined person does not have unhealthy habits. It's moderation in all things. You view the body as the temple in which all things happen. Energy levels are more dynamic if you maximize your health. I don't mean to imply that if you have some illness, you are not self-disciplined. But you should try to maximize your energy levels to what is possible for you.

It takes a self-disciplined manager to be a diplomatic leader, because patience is required. An individual lacking self-discipline is more likely to be impulsive, to shoot from the hip, to be an autocratic manager. Some may consider the concept of self-discipline and the ability to be a democratic leader a contradiction. In the words of George Caspar Homans, "Liberty is a beloved discipline." So, the less self-disciplined you are, the more likely you are to be autocratic. The more self-disciplined you are, the greater the likelihood that you can be a diplomatic leader.

To paraphrase Theodore Roosevelt, the best executive is one who has sense enough to pick good people to do what needs to be done, and self-restraint enough to keep from meddling with them while they do it. To do this requires restraint on the part of the manager and self-discipline on the part of the people, doing what needs to be done.

A self-disciplined person does not engage in mindless gossip with or about employees, or anyone for that matter. Of course it's acceptable to engage in small talk once in a while. Small talk is the lubricant of conversation and friendship, and it indicates that you're one of the group.

Also, too many new managers, in their spirit of accomplishment, think their position is more exalted than it is. This is true for the first-time manager all the way up to chief executive officer. The power of the job or authority is temporary. Eventually, we surrender it all, either willingly or reluctantly. I suspect this is why some "job-consumed" executives have difficulty retiring—the authority of the job and the perks are too important to them. Authority is simply one tool in the manager's toolbox. The self-disciplined manager will recognize that fact and not wallow in self-importance.

Benjamin Franklin, though addressing the matter of tact, offers a valuable lesson in self-discipline for the manager: "Remember not only to say the right thing in the right place, but far more difficult still, to leave unsaid the wrong thing at the tempting moment." This statement has a direct bearing on the relationship between managers and employees.

Every manager will face a crisis occasionally. Out of exasperation, the manager is tempted to strike out and say something tactless or mean-spirited. While at the time this may seem like a small thing, it is one of the larger temptations a manager faces. In potentially explosive situations, self-discipline must overtake the urge to speak out impulsively. You must do as Franklin writes, ". . . leave unsaid the wrong thing at the tempting moment."

Such a crisis will be a test of your self-discipline, but if the situation does get the best of you, and you regret something you've said, make it right as soon as possible. Do not allow it to fester. Too many managers have trouble saying, "I'm sorry" or "I was wrong."

In short, how you practice self-discipline in your career (and the rest of your life, for that matter) will build the foundation for dealing with the crises we must all eventually face.

25

"How Am I Doing?"

My comments to this point should have convinced you that I believe you have a fairly high opinion of your own capacities, and that it's not an inflated point of view. Having a realistic opinion of your own ability is not an ego problem if it's a proper assessment of your situation.

It seems to me that people get awfully mixed up in dealing with this ego thing. There are always people around who want you to feel guilty if you have a healthy opinion of yourself. Rather, it is "love your neighbor as yourself." This implies that your capacity to love your neighbor is determined by your capacity to love yourself. I think the principle applies to management, too.

Your Self-Image

Many excellent books have been written on the subject of self-image, and they have important concepts in them for the manager. Perhaps I can share a few basics that I believe will help you in your managerial career.

The fact is, we fall or rise by our self-image. If we have a low opinion of ourselves and believe we're going to fail, our subconscious will try to deliver that result to us. Conversely, if we have a high opinion of ourselves and think we're going to succeed, our chances for success are greatly increased. I realize that's an oversimplification, but it conveys the thought. If you think success, if you look successful, if you're confident of being successful, you greatly increase your chances to be successful. It's primarily a matter of attitude. If you believe you're a failure, that's what you're likely to be.

To reinforce a successful attitude you need some success along the way. Now that you've moved into your first managerial position, every success you have will serve as a building block to further achievements.

It should be obvious that you can't substitute feelings of success for actual accomplishments. You can't have the appearance without any substance. That would be a sham. You'll soon be found out, and to your own disadvantage.

An Impression of Arrogance

One of the most serious problems that I've observed in newly appointed young managers is the impression they give of arrogance. Be careful that you don't handle your feeling of success so that it's misconstrued as arrogance. A manager can feel pride in having been elevated into the managerial ranks without appearing cocky and arrogant. Rather, the impression conveyed should be one of *quiet confidence.*

Do you suspect that there are people in your organization who don't believe you were the right selection and who'd delight in your failure? That's not only possible, it's quite likely. An appearance that can be construed as arrogance is going to convince these people that they're correct in their assessment of you.

Skittish About Mistakes

In carrying out your duties as a manager, you'll make an occasional mistake. You'll exercise bad judgment. It happens to all of us. How you view and handle these mistakes is important to your own development and also in how others perceive you. Be completely honest with yourself, and everyone you associate with. Don't try to cover up a mistake, rationalize it, or—worse—imply that it might be someone else's fault. As mentioned earlier, too many managers have trouble getting two statements out of their mouths—it's as though they are stuck in the throat and can't be expelled. They are: "I made a mistake" and "I'm sorry." These statements are not signs of weakness. They are signs of confidence in your humanity.

New executives have difficulty accepting responsibility for the mistakes of people who report to them. So skittish are such managers about mistakes that they avoid criticism by handling the more complex work themselves. When they do this, they shut off their promotion possibilities, and kill themselves with overwork, which is literally a grim prospect.

The way to solve this problem is to build your entire managerial role. You become and select better trainers; you become a better selector of people; you develop better internal controls that minimize the mistakes and their impact. And when the mistakes happen, and you're the culprit, you admit it, correct it, learn from it, and—above all—don't agonize over it. Then you and the staff move on.

Self-Infatuation and Self-Contradiction

You have to put forth your best image, but don't be so successful at it that, like the movie star, you fall for your own publicity. Be willing to admit to yourself what your shortcomings are. You'd be surprised at how many executives can't do that. They of course have shortcomings. They can't be experts at everything. But in ascending to their exalted position, they find that everyone starts catering to them. It takes an unusual executive to realize that all that honorific treatment doesn't increase intelligence or boost knowledge. It's easy and pleasant to sit back and accept all that bowing and scraping. The executive is soon convinced that the adoration is deserved. Perhaps the charisma you think is personal is created by the position you hold.

The *infallibility syndrome* becomes most noticeable at the level of chief executive officer. Between the beginning manager and the top post are varying degrees of infallibility that seem to go with the job. You have to keep an honest perspective on who you are. If tomorrow you were named CEO, you wouldn't automatically become smarter than you were yesterday. But people would start listening to you as though you were one of the Three Wise Men. You didn't get smarter; you just gained more power. Don't confuse the two!

Pay little attention to what executives say in this regard. Pay more attention to what they do. If an executive says, "I hire people who are smarter than I am," think about what he does. Do all the people he hires seem to be clones of himself? If an executive says, "I encourage my people to disagree with me. I don't want to be surrounded by yes men," remember what happened last week when the executive snapped the head off of a subordinate who did express a different point of view. If an executive says, "My door is always open," and then looks visibly upset when you walk in saying, "Do you have a moment?" the words ring hollow, indeed. The words are contradicted by the action and the attitude.

Throughout your business life you'll encounter executives who espouse beautiful management philosophies. The main problem is that they wield their authority using other, less desirable concepts. So be honest with yourself; recognize who you are and try to get your performance to reflect your philosophy.

Shortcomings and Prejudicial Mind-Sets

I don't recommend advertising your weaknesses. That's foolish, but be willing to admit them to yourself and do all you can to correct them. For example, I've always found that the things I don't do well are also the things I don't enjoy. That's hardly a coincidence. But you'll get through those chores you don't like if you exercise some self-discipline and get them out of the way. Remember that, in your performance appraisal, the quality of your work will not excuse errors in the tasks you don't like. So, even the tasks you don't care for demand quality performance. Every job has aspects to it that you're not going to like; get them done well, so they are out of the way and you can get to the parts that are fun.

Be willing to admit mind-sets or attitudes of yours that may be a problem. You can't take the edge off them if you can't admit them. For example, I have a prejudice against second-generation wealth. Maybe it's envy. I'm convinced that if these people had to start at the bottom like the rest of us, they would fail. That's a prejudice; it's a mind-set. It's not provable; it's an emotional feeling I have. In dealing with such financially endowed individuals, I must be aware of my mind-set and make every effort to overcome it—but without overcompensating for it. It's a tough situation, but we must first be willing to admit a fault before we can deal with it.

Your Objectivity

Through the years I've known a great number of managers who tell you they're looking at a problem objectively, and then proceed to explain their attitudes or solutions in a most subjective way. When a manager starts off by claiming to be completely objective, you must wonder why the statement is being made. Does he protest too much? His preamble is a giveaway.

It's unlikely that you will ever be able to be completely objective. We are the sum of all of our experiences. We like some of our staff better than others, and you may not even be able to explain why. It could be personal chemistry. As long as you recognize that, you can compensate by dealing fairly with those who are less liked.

It seems better for the manager to not even bring up the subject of objectivity or subjectivity. How about being as honest as you can be in your dealings with people, and not get into all the shadings of objectivity and subjectivity? I think the recognition of how difficult it is to be completely objective is a great place to begin.

When your supervisor asks you, "Are you being objective?" your answer ought to be, "I try to be." No one can guarantee that he or she is completely objective, but the effort in that direction is laudatory.

Quiet Confidence

Develop quiet confidence in your decision-making ability. As you make more and more decisions, you will get better at it. Most management decisions do not require Solomon-like wisdom; they require the ability to develop the facts and know when you have enough information to make the decision. We covered this in some detail in Chapter 3. Most management decisions are based on common sense.

Don't make emotional decisions and rationalize them afterward. When you do, you will find yourself defending a decision that you wish you hadn't made. A bad decision is not worth defending, even if you're the person who made it. Once you rationalize a bad decision, you're trapped.

Too many new managers believe that they have to be fast decision makers in order to be successful. This creates an image of shooting from the hip, which is not a desirable image to foster. The other extreme is not getting your gun out of the holster. Balance and moderation are the keys. You don't want your staff saying, "She makes decisions too quickly," nor do you want them to say, "She has trouble making decisions." If your employees and your own manager were to rank your decision-making style, what you're after is, "just right."

Promotion and Self-Promotion

As mentioned in Chapter 7, you're judged by the performance of your area of responsibility. The people who report to you are more important to your future than the people you report to. That leads directly to the matter of office politics. It exists everywhere. People recoil at the idea of office politics, and that's because politics and politicians are not held in high regard by all people. One of the meanings of *politics*, which certainly has a positive spin, is, "the total complex of relations between people in society." The game of office politics exists, and nearly everyone plays it. The manager who doesn't play it is unknown to me. You're either a player or a spectator. Most managers are players.

Office Politics: Playing the Game

Some people are viewed as "cold turkeys" by those who report to them but as "warm, generous human beings" by their superiors. Such people are really playing the game, but in the long run they're sure to fail. However much they may succeed in fulfilling their ambitions at the office, they'll fail as human beings.

If getting promoted is more important to you than your integrity, than being your own person, then I would recommend that you skip the rest of this chapter because you won't like much of what is said in it.

I maintain that almost anyone can succeed temporarily by being an opportunist, but consider the price that's been paid in getting there. Granted that many of the decisions made about promotions will not seem fair to you, and that they won't all be made on the basis of ability. No one guaranteed you that life would be fair, so don't expect it.

I'm not saying that most promotions are made on the basis of something other than fairness and ability. But even though most companies do try to make these decisions fairly, it doesn't always come off that way. Besides, a decision that seems perfectly rational to the executive making it may not seem rational to you, especially if you thought you were the likely candidate for the promotion.

In spite of that, to get promoted you still have to prepare yourself for it. If you depend on luck or serendipity, your chances are greatly diminished. You have everything to gain and nothing to lose by being prepared. Who knows, your opportunity for promotion may come from outside your company. You want to be prepared for that possibility too.

Preparing Your Understudy

As soon as you've mastered your job, you must start looking for an understudy. The reason for this is clear. If the company refuses to consider candidates to replace you, it may view you as indispensable in your current position and you may be passed up for promotion.

Finding the appropriate understudy can be a delicate matter. You should not select your crown prince or princess too early. If the candidate doesn't develop properly and fails to demostrate the skills needed to move into your job, you could have a serious problem at hand. Changing your mind about a successor you've already selected is like opening a can of worms.

How you go about preparing for your own replacement is of critical importance. If you already have an assistant who's perfectly capable in the job, then it's a matter of helping that assistant develop as thoroughly and as rapidly as possible.

Give your assistant bits and pieces of your job to perform. Under no circumstance should you delegate your entire job to your assistant and then sit back and read newspapers and business magazines. The company obviously didn't put you in the position for that purpose.

Allow your assistant to do more and more aspects of your job until most of it has been learned. Make sure the assistant does each section of the job frequently enough that it won't be forgotten. Occasionally, invite the assistant to participate in the interviewing process when you're hiring new employees.

Assuming the assistant is performing satisfactorily, start your political campaign for your prospective replacement. Make sure your boss knows how well the man or woman is developing. On performance appraisals, use such terms as "promotable" and "is developing into an outstanding management prospect." Of course, never say these things if they're untrue; that would probably work to the disadvantage of both you and your assistant. But if the assistant is developing well, communicate it up to the next level without being blatant about it.

You run the risk that the assistant might get promoted out from under you. It's of course a risk worth taking. Even if this happens to you several times, you'll get the reputation of being an outstanding developer of people. That will add to your own promotability. Besides, you'll find that developing subordinates can be a very highly satisfying experience. And while you're worrying about preparing your people for promotion, it's hoped that your own boss is just as concerned about you and your future.

Multiple Choice

If you don't have an assistant already in place, you should assign parts of your job to several people and see how they run with the added responsibility and the new opportunity. This is indeed to your advantage, since training several replacements at once makes it unlikely that all the candidates will get promoted out from under you. This in-depth backstopping will serve you well in emergencies.

Don't be in too big a hurry to move a single candidate into the position of assistant. The moment you name a person as your assistant, others stop striving for the job. That's the trouble with any promotion. Those who don't get it stop aspiring to it, and that usually has an adverse effect on their performance, even though it may be temporary.

Here's a management concept that may be of value to you: Always hold something out for your subordinates to aspire to. If you get to the point where you have to select a single subordinate as your heir apparent, then let the losing candidates know that opportunities still exist for them in other departments, and that you'll help them toward their goal of a promotion.

But as long as you continue to have several prospects vying for the position, you must treat them as equals. Rotate the assignments among them. Make sure that all of them get exposed to all aspects of your job. If you're gone from the office occasionally, put each in charge of the operation in turn. Give them all a chance at managing the personnel aspects of the job too.

On some regular basis, meet with all the candidates at once and discuss your job with them. Don't say, "Let's discuss my job"; rather, talk about some specific problems they've encountered. All of them will benefit from the discussion. If one of them had to face an unusual management problem in your absence, why shouldn't all of them profit from the experience?

The Perils of Indispensability

Again let me point out the importance of not allowing yourself to become indispensable. Some executives trap themselves into this kind of situation. In their effort to ensure the quality of the work, they request that all difficult questions be referred to them. It doesn't take long for employees to figure out that anything out of the ordinary will soon be going to you as the boss. It isn't the time taken from your day that creates problems. The more fundamental trouble is that your people soon stop trying to work out the more complex problems by themselves.

I believe it's important that your people be encouraged to find answers on their own. They'll be better employees for it. There are limits, of course, to the areas of responsibility that can be delegated to them, but I've always felt that you're better off erring on the side of too much latitude in delegating responsibility than too little. I think it's good management to allow staff members some responsibility while still assuring them that the executive is accountable for their performance.

I'm sure you've heard people worrying about whether the company would get along without them while they're on vacation. They have it backward: Their real worry is that the company *will* get along just fine without them. The executive who's doing the right kind of job in developing employees and backup management can leave with the assurance that the department will function very smoothly in his or her absence. The truly efficient and dedicated executive, indeed, has progressed to the point where he or she can even be gone permanently—to a promotion in another company. I've known managers who, in a misguided view of what their job required, made themselves indispensable and spent the rest of their business careers proving it—by never being moved from that position.

The main problem with such people is that they don't understand what the job of management is about. Management isn't doing—it's seeing that it's done.

Your Predecessor

It helps a great deal if your predecessor in the job was a real dunderhead, who left the place in a shambles. Unless you're a complete loser, you'll look like a champion by comparison.

That's preferable to stepping into a smooth-running operation. Following a company hero who is retiring or who died in office is difficult because, no matter how well you perform, it's tough to be compared with a hero and the legend that time bestows upon him.

So if you ever have a choice between moving into an area of chaos or assuming a nice, clean operation, go with the disaster. It could be a great opportunity to establish a reputation that will stay with you your entire career. You'll not regret it.

Continuing Your Education

In preparing yourself for promotion, consider extending your knowledge of the business you're in. It's not enough to become expert in your restricted area of responsibility. You must understand more about your company's entire operation.

You can acquire this additional knowledge in several ways. For instance, you can broaden your knowledge through selected readings. Your own boss may be able to recommend published material that fits closely into your own company's operation and philosophy. No boss is ever insulted when asked for advice. However, a word of caution: Don't ask for advice too often, because your boss will either suspect you can't make up your own mind about too many things or figure you're seeking a favor. Neither of these reactions will help your cause.

If your company offers education programs, sign up for them. Even if you can't see any immediate benefit from them, they'll serve you well over the long haul. In addition, you're displaying an eagerness to learn.

Dressing for Success

Styles come and go, so what's inappropriate for business today may seem satisfactory in a couple of years, or even months, down the road. As a manager, you should not try to be a trendsetter by wearing far-out, extreme, avant-garde clothing.

You might not think it fair, but you will not advance your career if some executive refers to you, in conversations, as that "kooky dresser down on the first floor."

What is acceptable or extreme may vary by the kind of business you are in or the area of the country. For instance, what might work in a fashion magazine's office would seem inappropriate in a tradition-bound life insurance company. What my be acceptable in the southwestern part of the country may not sit well in the East. Obviously, what you wear as manager in a factory is altogether different from what you wear in an office. My primary point is that if you are going to be successful, it helps if you look successful—but not extreme. You should make a quiet statement, not a loud clatter.

If my wife and I are going for a day of shopping, we dress up, as the phrase goes, even though we live in laid-back California. There are two reasons: (1) we enjoy being well dressed, and (2) we are treated better in every establishment we enter. It may not be fair, but it's a fact. You'll make fewer fashion boo-boos as a businessperson by being a bit overdressed than by being underdressed. If I go to an event with a suit and tie on, and I find it's casual when we arrive, I can always take off my jacket and tie. If I go casually and find that everyone is in a suit and tie, I cannot easily add the apparel to get in compliance.

A rule of thumb is this: If you're not sure what to wear, you're better off erring on the side of overdressing.

Tooting Your Own Horn, but Softly

You can be the greatest thing since sliced bread, but if you're the only one who knows it, you won't go anywhere with your many talents. You need to get the word to persons you report to, in the most effective way possible.

If you're obviously tooting your own horn, people are going to react negatively. You may come off as a blowhard—a reputation you do not need. There are people with a great deal of ability who are too blatant in their self-promotion. It turns people off and has the exact opposite effect of the intended result.

You must be subtle. You want the reaction of effectively communicating.

Here's an example of how a situation might be handled so as not to be offensive to others and not generate a negative reaction: Let's say the local community college is offering courses that you think might help you do your job better, and thereby make you more promotable. Here are some ways to make sure your boss and the company are aware of your educational efforts. (Anything that gets the job done without overkill is what we're after.)

• Send a note to the human resources department, with a copy to your boss, asking that your personnel records show that you're taking the course. That puts the information in your file, where anyone examining your record and looking at candidates for promotion will see it. Upon completing the course, again notify HR, this time of the successful conclusion.

• Engage in casual conversation with your boss (if he hasn't acknowledged the copy of the note to HR), with, "One of the students in my accounting class said something funny last night. . . ." The boss may ask, "What accounting class?"

• Place the textbooks on your desk. Eventually the desired question may be asked.

• Ask your boss for clarification of a class discussion item that you did not fully understand.

• If you have a classmate to the office for lunch, introduce her to your boss. "Mr. Jones, I'd like you to meet my accounting classmate, Nelda Smith."

You get the idea. The more subtle you are, the less likely it is that your efforts will come off as braggadocio. Your boss, who knows something about self-promotion, recognizes that you are communicating about your accomplishments. If you do it well, he may even admire your style.

With an apology to the Bible, "What profit it a man if he becometh the most qualified new manager in the company if no one knoweth it?" Too few bosses will approach you and say, "Tell me—what are you doing to prepare yourself for promotion?" So you have to help them.

Some executives espouse the philosophy that if you do a great job, the promotions and raises will take care of themselves. This is a risky strategy, and you can't afford to take such chances. If your superiors don't know what you're doing, how can your accomplishments be taken into consideration? Develop a style of communicating the important aspects of your development, but do it with a degree of understatement so that others are not offended or construe you as too pushy.

But Is the Game Worth the Candle?

Being an outstanding manager and concurrently working up to the next rung on the ladder is a constant in almost every executive's career—unless you lose interest in moving higher. There's nothing wrong with not wanting to pay the price of moving to the next level. That's healthy if it's what you feel, because it means you're in touch with yourself. We all may reach a point where we are no longer considered promotable. Also, we may still be considered promotable, but we are comfortable where we are and don't want the aggravation that goes with the next promotion. Besides, the promotion pyramid gets much narrower the closer it gets to the top. Even the chairman and CEO are no longer promotable—at least in the present company.

In earlier editions of this book I mentioned that you have a right to know where you stand, as far as promotability is concerned. I even suggested that there was nothing wrong with *pressing* for that information. I have rethought that concept, and have changed my mind. If you don't care to be promoted, why ask? If you're offered a promotion, that's flattering and you might even change your mind.

If you care to be promoted, and you think a promotion is long overdue, why ask and have some boss say, "No, I don't believe you are promotable," or have her dodge the question and leave you unsatisfied? If you ask, and your boss puts a note in your file like, "Manager Jones pressed me about promotion. Told him, 'he's topped out.' " Now, let's say your boss leaves and goes to another company, and you're getting along famously with the new executive. You'd rather not have that "he's topped out" comment in your file. Why trigger that possible response—which may be faulty—and have it carved in stone?

If you are desirous of additional promotions, it helps to keep your eye on the ball and not be distracted by some future possibility. The greatest favor you can do to your career is be outstanding at the job you hold right now. Mastering your current job is your first priority. Every other ambition must be secondary to that objective.

Acquiring a Sponsor

It helps to have a boss who sings your praises at the executive level. Develop good relationships with all the executives you come in contact with, who know the quality of your performance, and who recognize your healthy upbeat attitude. If the only one who thinks highly of you is your boss, and she leaves the company for some super job in another organization, you've lost your advocate—unless she offers you a great job in her new company. It helps if your name is known positively by *many* executives in the organization. Being sponsored by several star executives is a great thing. Gladly accept any committee assignment that puts you in contact with managers and executives beyond your own department.

Style and Merit

Achieving the objectives discussed in this chapter requires satisfactory performance on your part and confidence in yourself. Often, the difference between a satisfactory job and a great job is image or style. I believe your style colors a superior's perception of your performance, especially if the style is one your superior reacts positively to. But a bad or offensive style is similarly critical in evoking a negative response.

Doing a great job and maximizing the mileage you get out of that is one thing; conning people into thinking you're doing an outstanding job when you're not cutting the mustard is quite another and will create problems. The message and the performance must be synchronized.

26

Organizing Your Own Time

Have you ever gone home from the office with the feeling that you didn't accomplish any of the things you wanted to get done that day? We all have days like that, spent entirely in putting out brushfires. Sometimes it can't be helped, but if it's happening to you regularly, part of the problem may be your own lack of organization.

My Own Approach

My own approach toward the first edition of this book is a good example. Almost every day, I'd set a goal of writing a full chapter, yet an entire week would go by without my having written a single line. The reason was my perception of needing to block out several hours for a chapter. Nothing was happening. Then I decided to break my goal down into smaller segments. The goal became to write two handwritten pages each day. Occasionally, I'd miss a day; then I'd set a goal of four pages for the next day. If for some unforeseen reason I missed more than two days, I did not make the goal a cumulative one, or I'd be right back to the block I had with the entire chapter.

As a result of setting more reasonable goals, I started getting material written, even though other demands on my time remained unchanged. The only change was my attitude toward, and approach to, the problem. One evening I sat down to write my two pages and ended up writing a dozen. If I had established a goal for that day of twelve pages, I would not have begun to write, owing to the lateness of the hour.

The List

A number of years ago I read an article about the late American industrialist Henry Kaiser. Among his many achievements was the establishment of a company that built cargo vessels called Liberty ships during World War II. These ships were completely constructed in a matter of days, truly a spectacular accomplishment.

The first thing Kaiser did on entering the office in the morning was to sit at his desk with a legal-size pad on which he listed the items he wished to accomplish that day. I don't recall that he attempted to list them in a priority order. During the day, the list remained on top of the desk. As a goal was accomplished, a line was drawn through it on the pad. Goals that didn't get accomplished that day would be put on the next day's list.

I tried this simple approach to organizing my day and was pleasantly surprised at how much more I started to accomplish. You're forced to plan the day's activities as you write the day's objectives on the pad. That's probably the greatest value of the technique.

There's one modification you might make in this system, however, that may make it even more useful. You know your own body better than anyone else. If you're at the peak of your energy levels early in the day (a morning person), you should do the tasks that require high energy the first thing each day. On the other hand, if you don't hit your stride until later in the day (an evening person), try to match the tasks to your different energy levels. It also helps to do the things you don't care for when you are at your higher energy times.

Some people prefer to rank items and do them in that order. I think it's unnecessary. After all, it's your list. You know what's urgent. I know of people who make three lists: Must Do, Have to Do, and Nice to Do. If you need that kind of regimentation, go for it. But such a regimented day has never been possible for me. I can't control the interruptions. I can't shut off the telephone. So I just make my little daily list of every variety of objectives, from dealing with emergencies to planning long-range projects that I'm hoping to get around to someday. Included are matters that are putting no pressure on me at the moment.

Another reason for not breaking my list down into categories is my knowledge of what has to be done immediately and what can wait. Let's face it, I know I can't survive as a manager if I ignore my emergencies. So even if the emergency is number twenty on my list, I'm not going to take care of nineteen other tasks ahead of the panic item.

Anyone else looking at my list would probably think I had lost my mind, because I write objectives down as they enter my head without worrying about any order or priority for accomplishing them. I'll even put personal items on the list, like reminding myself that I'm supposed to stop at the grocery store for a loaf of bread on my way home. A long-range project may appear on my list every day for a couple of months. Eventually, I'll get tired of repeatedly listing it and I'll get it done. I start feeling like a procrastinator if I keep it on my list too long.

I also get a psychological lift in drawing a line through the tasks that have been completed. I use a big marking pen. It's great to sit there at the end of the day's activities and see those big marks crossing off so many tasks. It's a feeling of deserved accomplishment.

And don't throw the list away when you leave the office. The next morning, yesterday's list will serve two purposes. It will remind you of all you accomplished the day before—there's nothing wrong with that—and will inform you of what remained unaccomplished. These latter items then go on the new list. That's especially important for long-range projects that might get accidentally dropped from the list. Too many creative ideas and projects get away from us because we didn't write them down.

Have you ever gone to bed with an office problem on your mind, only to wake up in the middle of the night with a solution? Then you awaken in the morning and it's gone. You can't retrieve the idea from your memory. A paper and pen on your nightstand for jotting such thoughts down during the night solves such retrieval problems.

The Closed Period

Some organizations follow a "closed-office" procedure you may want to use in mapping out your own day to accomplish more. For example, an office will have a two-hour-closed period, where it's business as usual except that no one in the office goes to see anyone else. No one makes interoffice phone calls and no company meetings are ever scheduled during this closed period. Genuine emergencies are handled expeditiously; calls from clients, customers, or other outsiders are accepted.

The idea has a great deal of merit. It means you'll have two hours each day when no one from within the company is going to call you on the phone or come into your office. It gives you an opportunity to control what you do during the specified period. Perhaps some person got the idea while working in the office on a weekend and noticing how much more was accomplished then than in the same period of time during the week. But the idea is feasible only if you don't shut off your customers or clients during the closed period. It's an idea an entire organization can use to advantage.

Remembering and Reflecting

Here's a bit of advice that won't do a whole lot for you at the office but will help you remember things you're supposed to stop for on the way home. Put a reminder in the pocket where you keep your car keys. Then, on your way to the parking lot at the end of the workday, you'll reach into your pocket for the car keys and presto!—there it is. Maybe you don't get distracted from doing personal errands the way I do; you may therefore not need to have such reminders. I do.

A final suggestion or two about how to best organize your time. Plan to have a quiet period each day. You may not get it every day, but it's important that you set aside some time for daydreaming and reflection. It's vital to the inner person. Also, problems that seem insurmountable often ease into proper perspective during these quiet times.

And try to put each day's activity into proper context. A friend kept one of those "one day" calendars next to the door of his office. Beneath it sat a solitary, empty wastebasket. As he left the office at the end of the day, he would tear off the sheet for the day just ending. He stood above the wastebasket and tore that "day" into as many small pieces as he could, then watched the small pieces slowly flutter down into the wastebasket below. When I asked him what his thoughts were as he went through this ritual, he said, "It symbolizes to me that this day is over. I've done the best I can with it. I now go on to the other segments of my life, leaving this day behind, where it belongs." Not a bad way of letting the completed workday slip into quiet repose.

27

The Written Word

It's a source of amazement and some amusement that many articulate people are reduced to blubbering incompetents when required to put their thoughts on paper.

Some people are intimidated by a blank sheet of paper and a pen (or typewriter). Let's examine why this feeling of panic overtakes individuals who otherwise appear to be competent and confident.

First, we have the *test syndrome*. Some people panic when taking examinations. All they have is that blank sheet of paper and the material inside their head, which must be "up" to translating information to paper. Pass or fail depends on what is scratched on that threatening blank sheet.

Another reason people may not feel confident about using the written word is that they do not read much themselves. They get through what they consider required reading, but they don't read for pleasure. Instead, they watch television, which is more passive than reading. You don't learn much about good writing by watching television. Clearly, television is not to be blamed for all the social ills attributed to it. However, few would quarrel that it has lessened the time spent reading, which in turn has had an adverse effect on many people's interest in writing.

The telephone also plays a part in discouraging the written word. Although most of us (unless we are employed by a phone service) would like to see less expensive phone bills, the fact is that it is relatively inexpensive to make a long-distance phone call today. This was not the case for previous generations. A long-distance phone call was a luxury most could not afford, even if they had a telephone. People wrote letters instead, and it cost only three cents to mail them. Today very few people under age 40 write letters. People communicate with distant friends by telephone. It's a more intimate and satisfying way of communicating, but it has destroyed the art of letter writing.

People who spell poorly are usually aware of the fact and don't want to look foolish by demonstrating it. So they avoid writing. There's an easy solution to this excuse.

Every secretary is familiar with "word books." They are like dictionaries except there are no definitions. You go to a word book to get the correct spelling. It's the reason most people go to the dictionary. A word book is simply more convenient. It's small and easy to hide in the middle drawer of your desk. I'm a better than average speller, but I keep two of them—one at my office and one in my den at home. They remove an obstacle to writing.

Another reason for using a word book is a situation that occurs to all of us who put thoughts on paper. Suddenly a word that we've known all our lives looks wrong to us. A word book is a quick way to put the mind at ease. (I'd like to have five dollars for every time over the years that I've gone to my word book because *occurs* all of a sudden looks funny to me.)

Because people don't write much, they are intimidated when they do have to write. An analogy to public speaking might make the point. If you seldom give a speech in public, you are probably intimidated by the situation. And when you are intimidated, you are not relaxed. You are uptight and nervous. Your manner of speaking is stiff and uncomfortable. You communicate your apprehension to the audience; people may even feel uncomfortable for you. Your manner destroys their confidence in you and in the truth or wisdom of the message you are trying to deliver.

The same thing happens with a written communication. If you are intimidated by the situation, your writing will be stiff and stilted. Under such circumstances, you may try to cover the situation by writing in a more formal manner, using words you would never use in conversation with a friend.

Books and courses will tell you how to write business letters and interoffice memos. They can be a big help, provided you don't take on the characteristics of the person who wrote the course. Your goal is to improve your technical skills, not to change your personality.

Mental Imagery Helps

My suggestion for improving your writing skills is to use mental imagery. Instead of being intimidated by the blank piece of paper, get a mental image of the person you are writing to. See that person in your mind. You might even go so far as to imagine the person seated in an easy chair at the office drinking a cup of coffee and reading your letter. Or you could visualize yourself sitting in a coffee shop telling the person the message you want to convey.

Imagine that you are having a conversation with the person in a friendly environment. Now speak. Use words you'd use in conversation. If you don't use four-syllable words in your conversation, don't use them in your written communication; they usually denote a feeling of inferiority. (Even if you do feel inferior about your writing, don't advertise it—keep it to yourself.)

When conjuring up the mental picture of the person you're writing to, always imagine a friendly face. Even if you are writing to someone you can't stand, imagine that you're writing to a friend. *Never* conjure up hostile feelings because they may come through in your writing. Imagining a friendly face will bring a friendly, warm tone to your communication.

Now let's take a broader situation: writing a memo to all the people in your department or division. You don't want to imagine forty-five people sitting in an auditorium waiting for you to speak. That's too formal a situation, and unless you're an outstanding and relaxed public speaker, the image is going to make your writing formal and uptight.

Instead, get a mental picture of two or three of the friendliest subordinates you have reporting to you. Imagine that you are on a coffee break or lunch break with them. Now say to them what you have to say. That's what you write. If you're writing to fellow managers in other departments, you can use similar mental images.

Now, let's assume you have to write a report or a memo to the president of the company, and let's assume you are scared to death of Ms. Big. Getting a mental image of the president is only going to make the situation worse. Think instead of your kindly aunt, the one who is your favorite. Imagine that relative as the president. Now write the letter. The tone will be altogether different.

Incidentally, no matter how informal your organization is, always address the president formally. Never address the president by his first name. At the end of the letter type your full name and title; sign just your first name if you wish. This suggests that although you show respect for the president and the office, you are not a stuffy person who expects such formality in return.

Writing informally does not mean using incomplete sentences or faulty grammar. You need to make certain your grammar is correct. It's the tone of the communication that I am concerned with.

If you are uncomfortable about your use of grammar in written communications, learn the basics. They are not that tough and they are certainly not cumbersome. An inexpensive book on grammar will help you in that regard. Don't rely on a secretary to backstop you in this area. That's the easy way out and may cause you to put off achieving competence in this important skill.

The reason I strongly recommend that your grammar be correct in writing is: If it isn't, there's a chance that it's also incorrect in your formal speaking and even in informal conversations. If that is the case, it may have an adverse impact on future promotion possibilities.

So do your best to write and speak the language correctly and to give it the dignity it deserves. Above all, remember—write to that friendly mental image.

28

The Telephone

Almost all of us have known people who in person are warm and friendly but for some reason sound brusque and unfriendly on the telephone.

You've probably heard the following statement (origin unknown): "You never get a second chance to make a first impression." If you make a bad first impression, who knows how long it may take to overcome it? Unfortunately, you may not know when you're creating a negative impression, especially on the telephone. What follows are some suggestions that may help the first-time manager develop some good phone habits.

Avoid Screening Your Calls

When a person moves into management there is a great temptation to start having all phone calls screened by an assistant. It's usually unnecessary, and is often an ego trip on the part of the new manager to appear important and busy.

Put yourself in the position of the caller. In most organizations the call comes through a switchboard, and the following dialogue occurs:

Operator: Good afternoon, the Acme Company.
Smith: May I speak to Mary Jones, the manager of Accounts Receivable?

176

Operator: One moment please [*or* I'll ring her].

[The call is put through and your assistant answers.]

Assistant: Ms. Jones's office.
Smith: [again]: May I speak to Mary Jones?
Assistant: I'll see if she's in. Who may I say is calling?
Smith: Lloyd Smith.
Assistant: May I tell her what it's about?
Smith: I want to see if she's received my check.

[The assistant comes back on the line in a minute or two.]

Assistant: I'm sorry, she's in a meeting. May I have her call you?

[If the caller isn't exasperated, he probably gives the number. About two hours later, the assistant phones back.]

Assistant: Mr. Smith please.
Smith: This is Lloyd Smith.
Assistant: Would you hold for Ms. Mary Jones? She'll be on the line in just a moment.

If Mr. Smith slams the phone in the assistant's ear, it is just what this egomaniacal procedure deserves.

I'm not suggesting that you always answer your own phone. Obviously if you're away from the area, someone must cover your calls. But when you're at your desk and not in conference, answer the phone when it rings.

Many callers who are asked by the assistant, "Who may I say is calling?" or "May I tell her what it's about?" may take these questions personally. They interpret them this way: "If I'm important enough, or the subject matter is big enough, maybe I'll get through." Unfortunately, that is the way many callers read such questions because many people do get the runaround on the telephone.

Place Calls Yourself

There is hardly any reason for having an assistant place phone calls for you. It takes longer for the assistant to place the call and then tell you that the party is on the line than it does to place the call yourself. With redial capabilities and the capacity to place frequently called numbers on an automatic dialer, I can think of few reasons to have calls placed for you.

One apparent reason why it is done is to play "big shot." It's a transparent ego trip. For example, I received a call one day from the secretary of a friend of mine, who was at the same level in the organization as I was. This was the fifth or sixth time this individual had left me holding the line for several minutes waiting for him to pick up the phone. The call came at a hectic time for me, and the conversation went like this:

Secretary: Mr. Belker, would you hold for Mr. Swanson?
Me: No I won't. *[I hung up the phone.]*

[A few minutes later, the phone rang and it was Swanson himself.]

Swanson: Loren old buddy, we must have been disconnected.
Me: No, we were not disconnected, ol' buddy. I hung up on you because my time is as valuable as yours.

Swanson never did that to me again. I don't know if he continued doing it with others. Of course, I don't suggest that you do this to anyone except your peers or people you may outrank. If a person outranking you does it, you'll need to grin and bear it, but you know it's an ego trip and doesn't say anything positive about that person.

It may be obvious that if you're going to make a business phone call, you ought to have any necessary file pulled and all required information at hand. The thought might occur to you that having an assistant screening calls provides an opportunity for the appropriate file to be pulled as the call is switched to you. That is true, but the poor impression the screening creates simply isn't worth it.

Every manager ought to have a buzzer connected to an assistant's desk so that when he is on the phone and needs a file pulled, the assistant can get it. Buzz the assistant and write on a pad, "Please pull the R. L. Schultz file." For this purpose, always keep two pads by your phone—one to make your own notes and the other to write notes to your assistant.

When you review your phone messages after having been away from the office or in a meeting, see which ones require the file to be pulled before returning calls. Or, an experienced assistant can do this even before you return.

Telephone Technique

Be sure your telephone voice sounds warm and friendly. A pleasant tone of voice is essential; any harshness will create a bad impression. People can't control the voices they were given, but they can practice sounding friendly, efficient, and businesslike. But take care not to go to the other extreme and sound gushy and saccharine sweet—it sounds phony.

Getting into the habit of smiling when you answer the phone will do wonders for your tone of voice. This isn't always easy to do—especially in the middle of a hectic day when the last thing you need is another interruption. But the person calling does not know that it's a bad time to call and does not deserve to be snapped at. Place a small mirror with a stand-up bracket next to your phone so that you can see yourself smile while you're on the phone. (The problem with leaving it on your desk permanently is that people will think you are narcissistic.)

Another way to improve your telephone voice is to have it recorded. A small contact microphone can be purchased at almost any sound or stereo shop for a few dollars. It plugs into the microphone connection on a cassette recorder. With this device in place, have a friend call you several times. Answer the phone in various ways: smiling, frowning, hurried, and so on. You can then hear what you sound like to others on the phone. If you're not used to hearing your recorded voice and are like most people, you probably won't like the way you sound. But if you don't record your voice, you can only guess how you sound, and you'll have no clue about the impression you make. Friends, unwilling to hurt your feelings, are unlikely to tell you if your voice is unpleasant. No matter how bad you

think you sound, you can improve your phone voice enough
to come across pleasantly on the telephone.

In Your Absence

In addition to your own phone manners and tone of voice, you
need to be concerned about how the phone is answered in
your absence, and in your area generally. When you are
outside the office, call in once in a while to find out how calls
are being handled.

A phone call that comes to your office in your absence
ought to be answered, "Ms. Abernathy's office" or "Mr. Tay-
lor's office." Even if the style of your office is casual, the phone
call may be from someone outside the company, so the more
formal approach should be used. If the approach is too casual,
the customer may think you will be too casual with his concerns too. How would you like to be wheeled into the surgical
suite and hear the janitor greet your surgeon, "Hi-ya Freddie"?

If you are at an early morning meeting, don't allow your
assistant to tell people that you aren't in yet. That makes it
look as if you don't get to work on time. Far better for him to
say, "Ms. Abernathy had a breakfast meeting downtown this
morning." Your assistant should always be told about the
meeting the afternoon before an early appointment. How much
you want to tell strangers on the phone is a matter of discretion.

Perhaps this is so obvious that it shouldn't be mentioned,
but sometimes the more obvious matters are overlooked. When
your assistant takes calls in your absence, he must always ask
for the phone number. Occasionally, a caller will say, "She
knows my number." In that case the assistant shouldn't push
for it. Before you return, however, the assistant ought to look
up the number on your phone listings.

It is important to indicate the time the call is received.
Most managers will look over all their phone messages, sort
out the emergencies, and return the rest in the order they were
received on a first-come, first-served basis.

29

The Grapevine

This chapter could be subtitled, "The Most Effective Communication." Any organization with more than five people has a grapevine. Grapevines come about because people communicate with each other, and people have a great need to know what's going on. If they don't know, they'll speculate about what's going on. You will never put an end to the grapevine, so you might as well accept its existence and the fact that its tentacles reach into all corners of the organization.

One way a manager can avoid much incorrect speculation is to do a good job of communication. If you do, they'll have less opportunity to speculate incorrectly about important matters. There will always be speculation and gossip. But by being an effective communicator, you can reduce the *incorrect* speculation. You'll never stop it completely, unless you have the power to impose vows of silence while people are at work, which isn't going to happen.

The grapevine even takes place after hours on the telephone. Such a phone call in the evening might go like this: "You didn't get to hear the latest of what's happening now. I heard you were at the dentist. You won't believe this but. . . ." And so it goes on, ad infinitum.

When I was a new manager, several of us were wondering how quickly and efficiently the grapevine could handle a rumor. We knew that one of the principal participants was on the fifth floor. I was to go to the fifth floor and tell this person an outrageous rumor that could be remotely possible. I would then walk back down the stairs to the first floor where my work area was. I was not gone ten minutes. When I got back to my desk, the secretary said, "You'll never believe what I just heard." She repeated the rumor I had delivered upstairs, with the addition of a few creative modifications.

Use the Grapevine Sometimes

As a manager you can tap into the grapevine, for both sending and receiving. If you develop good relationships with your people, they'll tell you what's going on. In fact, some of them will vie for the opportunity to be the first to bring you the latest scoop.

You can send messages via the grapevine, too. If you don't use it too often, it can be effective. The emphasis should be on direct communication with your staff, and in doing so, you avoid the embellishments that are invariably tacked on.

If you want to put something into the grapevine as a trial balloon, for example, a perfect opening is "Keep this under your hat, but . . ." or "This is highly confidential, but. . . ." That will ensure its rapid movement through the system. Remember, the only time an item is completely confidential is when you tell no one.

30

A Sense of Humor: A Trusted Friend

Many new managers take themselves much too seriously. Life is earnest, life is grim, and without a sense of humor, it is deadly. New managers have to learn not to take themselves too seriously and to develop a sense of humor.

One reason many of us take ourselves too seriously is because of the immediacy of the world in which we move. Our daily activities are important to us because they're the ones we know most intimately. Therefore, everything that happens at the office looms large in our lives. We should try to do our jobs to the best of our ability, but once we're sure in our own minds that we have done so, we shouldn't worry about it. The key phrase is *once we're sure in our own minds*. Most of us are our own severest critics.

Of course, the work we do is important. If it were not, no one would part with cold cash in return for our efforts. But we must keep what we do in perspective. It may be important in our office, and it may be important to the people who deal with our office, but it may not seem terribly significant when measured against the history of humankind. When you've had a bad day and all seems lost, remember that a hundred years from now no one will care, so why should you let it ruin your year, month, week—or evening, for that matter? Our jobs are important, but let's keep what we do in perspective.

The English author Horace Walpole (1717–1797) said "The

world is a comedy to those that think, a tragedy to those that feel." It's much easier not to take yourself too seriously if you have a sense of humor. Nearly everyone has some sort of sense of humor. But it is more keenly developed in some people than in others. Even if you feel your sense of humor is weak, you can improve it.

Developing a Sense of Humor

Here's a new flash that provides some hope. Many people who have a reputation for being funny, clever, and humorously creative don't really have any of these characteristics. What they have is a terrific memory and a sense of *appropriateness recall.* They can reach back into their memories quickly and find a humorous line they've heard or read that's appropriate to the situation at hand. They get a reputation for having a sense of humor, and they do have one, but they're not necessarily creative. It's much like the difference between perfect pitch, which some feel a person is born with, and relative pitch, which can be developed and practiced.

So you can develop a sense of humor by reading, by seeing the right kind of humorous movies, and by studying comedy. Watch television personalities who have a reputation for being funny. Watch people who are "ear funny." A cream pie in the face or a pratfall might be "sight funny," but you can't use these gags at the office, and seldom in your social life.

When my younger brother, Gene, was graduating from high school, he commented that with a couple hundred in his graduating class, nothing would set him apart from his classmates. I had a suggestion: "As you walk across the stage, stumble and fall on your face just as you get close to the area where you're handed your diploma. You'll get a big laugh, and you'll be fondly remembered at every class reunion for the rest of your life."

Fortunately, Gene did not take my advice, but he was thinking about it as he walked across the stage, and as a result he was grinning from ear to ear. That alone set him apart from most of the other graduates.

Humor—Not Sarcasm

Achieving a reputation for having a dry sense of humor is acceptable; acquiring a reputation as the office clown is not. I'm sure you appreciate the difference. Being witty is one thing; being a buffoon is quite another. But one warning: If you have never said anything funny at the office, break into humor on a gradual basis; otherwise someone will want to check the water supply.

Many people mistake sarcasm for wit; some sarcasm can be funny, but there's a twofold problem with being sarcastic. First, you achieve a reputation for being a cynic, which is not a welcome trait in the executive suite. Second, sarcasm is often funny at someone else's expense. You don't want people to think you prey on the weaknesses or idiosyncrasies of others. Also you don't want to offend someone and make an enemy. It's best if your humorous remarks point inward or are neutral in nature. Making fun of yourself or your own foibles makes you a self-deprecating wit, which offends no one. Trading insults with another person can be fun, but it's not a practice for beginners and therefore should be avoided.

Humor, the Tension Reliever

A sense of humor is most valuable when things become hectic and tense. A well-placed humorous remark can relieve the tension. It's like opening a steam valve so that the pressure can escape. It's healthy to see humor in tense situations. Even when it seems inappropriate to make your humorous remark aloud, thinking about it may put a smile on your face and keep you from getting a migraine.

We are surrounded by funny situations every day, but it takes a trained eye to see them. As with the beauty all around us, we don't look for them, and we may not even recognize them when we do see them. With practice, however, you'll begin to see the humor in what goes on all around you.

Finally, there's a compelling reason for not taking ourselves and this life too seriously: None of us is going to get out of it alive anyway.

31

Managing, Participating in, and Leading Meetings

In Chapter 26, mention was made of companies that have "closed periods" during which office personnel don't phone one another and don't attend meetings. That gives them a certain amount of uninterruptible time each day. Indeed, I have often thought the productivity of the entire country would be greatly increased if all office meetings of more than two people, is business and government, were banned for one year.

Advance Notice

An idea that helps generate a more productive meeting is to send the proposed agenda to committee members a few days before the meeting. Going to a meeting unprepared is counterproductive. Many meetings are spur-of-the-moment necessities, but a scheduled meeting should have an agenda.

If the chairman is the only person knowledgeable about what's going to be covered, that might feed the chairman's ego but it damages the quality of the meeting.

Your thoughts while reviewing the agenda might go along these lines: "What information do I need to vote intelligently on the required decisions? In what way can my particular experiences with the company provide valuable input to the entire committee? What points of view are the other members of the committee likely to bring to the meeting? Is the chairperson's point of view likely to prevail? Do I agree or disagree with it? Do I have a strong opinion on the subject, or do I need a lot more facts? Am I completely neutral on the issue? Are certain people on the committee going to fight for their position or is the entire committee likely to be neutral until the facts come out and the discussion develops?"

Mistakes Managers Make

Too many managers who are new to the committee process feel obligated to have an opinion on every issue. That isn't necessary. Have an opinion where your motivation is the issue, not the perceived need to speak. It's far better to make a few thoughtful statements than to rattle on about everything. It's preferable to have an executive attending the meeting say, "John is a thoughtful person," as opposed to, "You ask John the time, and he builds you a watch," or "He does rattle on, doesn't he?"

The other extreme of remaining silent during the entire meeting is just as bad. It implies you are intimidated by the situation and that is not an image to create. Even if the situation does intimidate you a bit, never let them see you sweat. The chapter on public speaking (Chapter 33) will help you in this regard.

Never say anything uncomplimentary in a meeting about anyone on your staff. It will be received as disloyalty on your part. Handle situations, not personalties. I've seen managerial careers halted by a manager who trashed an employee in front of a high-ranking executive. Such behavior says more about you than about the employee.

Some managers view a meeting with higher-ranking executives as a place to display management skills and wares. That is all right if you go about it correctly. However, if you view the meeting as a competition with other managers at your level, your emphasis is wrong. Your goal should be to be a productive, contributing member of the committee, not to show up other managers. Competition is the wrong element to bring to the table.

Another mistake too many managers make is seeing which way the boss is going on an issue, so that their positions are the same. The idea is that their bosses will think more of them if they agree with them, or think as they do. Most bosses immediately spot that game, and the managers may be thought of as spineless. Of course, if you have a point of view that is different from your boss, state it in a diplomatic, reasoned way—but you ought to do that anyway. If everyone agrees with the boss, you don't need the committee.

By the way, far too many managers lack the courage to take a position different from their bosses. I suspect that, in the vast majority of situations, the courage to state a thought-out position, even if different from the boss's, does more for a career than transparent agreement. I have known executives who have deliberately taken a false position to see which sheep would follow, and then agree with someone who had the courage to state the correct position. (Most executives didn't get to their exalted positions by being stupid.)

I served for many years on a job evaluation committee with the president of the company. There were five of us on that committee. The president very wisely didn't announce his score on each factor until after he'd called for everyone else's ranking. That approach precluded anyone from playing up to the president, if she would have been tempted to do so. Any executive chairing a committee with members she outranks would do well to hold back disclosing her own position until *after* everyone else has made a commitment. Such an executive does not need subordinates to play up to her. This approach might also teach junior managers that it is okay to have a different point of view. Of course, as mentioned earlier in this book, some executives say they don't want yes people, but their actions indicate otherwise. These executives end up with rubber-stamp committees that merely provide cover for the executive, and they are a terrible waste of corporate and managerial time.

Advantages of Committee Work

There are several advantages to being placed on a committee. First, someone believes you can make a contribution or you wouldn't have been selected. So make the most of it. Second, you may come in contact with managers and executives across a wide spectrum of the organization. These are valuable contacts. Third, you may have the opportunity to get involved in decisions that reach beyond your own area of responsibility. This broadens your experience with the organization as a whole.

Chairing a Committee

You may be placed in charge of a committee, and that is a compliment: Someone sees leadership in you. Don't shy away from such an opportunity.

Some of the best training for chairing a committee is in being exposed to some poorly chaired ones. Most meetings last too long. You can't help but wonder if some folks think sitting around at a meeting beats working. But probably the main reason meetings last too long is that they are poorly planned and inefficiently chaired.

In addition to the earlier suggestion about circulating an agenda in advance, distribute the minutes of the previous meeting. Most everyone then reads the minutes before they get to the meeting, and except for a minor correction now and then, approval of the minutes is quickly disposed of. Contrast that with everyone's sitting around for fifteen minutes reading the minutes and feeling compelled to nit-pick them to death.

Obviously, all agendas show starting times of meetings. It adds discipline to a meeting if you also show the expected closing time. People tend to stay focused on the subjects at hand if the meeting has an expected adjournment time.

Most committee meetings are run rather informally. You'll seldom chair a committee that requires you to be an expert parliamentarian. If it does get formal, you'll have to familiarize yourself with *Roberts Rules of Order*. Having this reference available is a good thought, but I suspect you'll rarely need it. In all the years I've attended and chaired business meetings, I can't recall any parliamentarian questions having been raised, except in jest.

The rules of common sense should prevail in chairing a meeting. Keep your cool. Don't let anyone press your panic button. Be courteous to everyone on the committee. Avoid putting people down. Act as a facilitator, not as a dictator. Keep to the subject. Don't cut people off before they've had their say, but don't allow them to drift away from the subject. Always deal with the problem at hand. A fair chairperson discourages the same points from being repeatedly expressed.

Don't get involved in personalities, even if others do. Be better organized than anyone else on the committee. Develop the kind of thoughtful relationships with people on the committee that will prompt them to come to you beforehand with unusual items, thereby avoiding unpleasant surprises. Be fair to everyone, even minority opinions that are unlikely to prevail. The majority view should not steamroller the minority opinion, at least until that opinion has had a fair hearing. If you are fair to all viewpoints, you'll earn the respect of the committee. Whether the chair votes on every issue or votes only to break ties will be determined by company tradition.

Being a successful committee chairperson is another chance to display the high quality of your management skills.

32

A Touch of Class

There are many meanings to the word *class*. The meaning we will concern ourselves with is "style and elegance in one's behavior." Class in a manager or executive consists of what is done and, often of greater importance, what is *not done.*

- Class is treating people with the dignity their humanity deserves. It is not in treating them as objects of production.
- Class has nothing to do with your social status in life. It has everything to do with your behavior.
- Class does not use foul language, even when irritated. Class does mean having the large vocabulary that makes four-letter words unnecessary.
- Class does not have to be the center of attention. It can allow others to bask in glory without feeling slighted.
- Class does not tell off-color or racially demeaning jokes.
- Class separates any sexual desires from the workplace, and would never make a remark to a person of the opposite sex that wouldn't be said in front of one's mother, if she were standing alongside.
- Class does not say anything derogatory about the organization, no matter how justified you may feel it is, at a moment of disappointment.
- Class does not allow the unsatisfactory actions or negative words of others to drag one down into that ugly arena.
- Class does not lose its cool. It never burns its bridges.

- Class does not rationalize mistakes. It learns from them and moves on.
- Class in a manager emphasizes *we* and downplays *I*.
- Class is good manners.
- Class means respect for oneself as a foundation for respect for others.
- Class never makes a demeaning remark about one's spouse. Such remarks say more about the speaker than the spouse.
- Class in a manager means loyalty to one's staff.
- Class means not believing one is superior to one's employees; each simply has different responsibilities.
- Class does not take action when angry. It waits until cool reason has returned. Class is not impetuous.
- Class recognizes that the best way to build oneself is to first build others.
- Class does not become overly concerned about receiving credit. Class also recognizes that sometimes one receives more credit than one deserves. It helps balance out those times when there are no accolades.
- Class works hard at making action consistent with words.
- Class doesn't build oneself up by tearing others down.
- Class leads by example.
- Class knows the importance and value of a warm smile.

33

The Role of Public Speaking in Your Career

I'm repeatedly amazed by the number of capable executives who can't handle a public speaking situation. Standing up there on the platform, they come off as the dullest clods imaginable. The impression the audience receives is that they're not very good on the job, either. That impression may not be correct, but as we've discussed earlier, people act based on their perceptions.

Prior Preparation

Many managers are rotten public speakers because they wait until they find themselves in a speaking situation before they do anything about it. By then it's too late. You can be the greatest manager in the world and your light will be hidden under a bushel basket if you don't prepare yourself to be a public speaker.

Because so few people in managerial positions prepare themselves to speak publicly, you'll have a leg up on most of them if you learn how it's done. Public speaking frightens many people, and so they avoid it like the plague. But what they probably don't consider early in their careers is that although speeches to outside groups may be avoided, the speech that will take place within their own office must be faced.

It may be a meeting of your department in which you have to get up and explain some new company policy. It may be a retirement dinner for someone in your area of responsibility, and you're expected to make a "few appropriate remarks." I've seen managers go to unbelievable lengths to avoid such speaking situations. They will use ploys such as arranging a business trip so they'll be out of town or scheduling their own vacation for that time. They'll spend the rest of their business lives plotting how not to get up in front of a group and speak. How much better off they'd be if they'd obtain the necessary skills and turn these negative situations into resounding pluses.

What many people don't realize is that learning to be an adequate public speaker will also improve their ability to speak extemporaneously. How do you respond when you're unexpectedly called on to say a few words? The most extreme example of someone who has difficulty in front of an audience is the person "who couldn't lead a group in silent prayer."

The close friend who first got me interested in public speaking is fond of saying, "Speech training won't get rid of the butterflies in your stomach, but it will organize them into effective squadrons."

Where to Receive the Speech Training

It seems appropriate at this point to mention a nonprofit organization that I believe will help you learn how to be a capable public speaker. I'm referring to Toastmasters International, a self-help organization dedicated to the concept of developing skills in listening, thinking, and speaking. There are neither professionals nor staff members in these clubs, only people who have a mutual interest in developing their speaking capacity. For a modest semiannual fee, you receive the manuals you'll need to begin the process. You go at your own speed, and you'll find a group of people who help one another not only by providing an audience but also be engaging in formal evaluation sessions.

Another aspect of the Toastmasters training that I think is invaluable is what is called "Table Topics." This part of the meeting is designed to develop your skills in extemporaneous speaking. The Topic Master calls on various people (usually those not scheduled to give a formal speech that evening) to talk for two or three minutes on a surprise subject. The time you have to prepare extends from the moment you rise from your chair until the moment you arrive at the lectern.

There are Toastmasters clubs all over the world, so it's likely that you'll find one in your area. If not, you can write to get information about a club close to you. The world headquarters address is Toastmasters International, 2200 N. Grand Avenue, Santa Ana, California 92711.

Obviously, since these clubs include all kinds of individuals, you'll find degrees of quality. But you'll probably gain benefit in direct proportion to the effort you put into it. Most of these clubs meet weekly. Some are dinner clubs and some are not. Naturally, the dinner clubs will cost more.

An innovation in the last two decades is the in-house Toastmasters Club. A company recognizing the value of having articulate managers and employees sponsors a club within the organization. It may meet over the lunch hour, before work starts, or after it ends. The approach has several advantages; one is the convenience and another is the company imprimatur of the concept. Accomplishments of the various members may be published in the company magazine, thereby bringing recognition to staff engaged in a self-improvement project.

I can think of some disadvantages of the in-house club. For one, you have people of various ranks participating. There may be a temptation to whitewash a speech evaluation of your boss. The boss might even say, "Evaluate me as you would anyone else," but some timid souls might have trouble doing that. Of course, this disadvantage might be offset by the fact that if you have higher ranking managers and executives in the club, they get a chance to know you and your accomplishments. People going through such self-improvement together do develop a long-lasting camaraderie. It's an important bond. If you have an in-house club, everyone must know that rank is left at the door, although that is often easier said than done.

The advantage of the outside club is that you have no rank problems, and you may not feel you are competing with fellow employees. You also come into contact with people from a wide variey of businesses and occupations, as opposed to everyone's working for the same company.

There are other ways to get speech training and experience. My recommendation of Toastmasters does not preclude other venues. Almost all community colleges offer such training. Some adult education courses offered by local high schools make such training available. The Toastmaster programs, the community colleges, and the adult education of local high schools are moderately priced. The Dale Carnegie Course is very good, although it is more expensive.

Fringe Benefits

How many outstanding public speakers do you personally know, either inside or outside your organization? I'll bet not many, if any. Why don't you resolve to be one of the few who are outstanding? Think of the possibilities not only for promotion within your company but for positions of leadership within the community. As a matter of fact, the opportunities for leadership challenges may come more quickly outside the company. Consider what that may open up for you. There are a lot of followers out there waiting for someone to lead them. One characteristic most outstanding leaders have is the ability to speak persuasively on public occasions. There's no reason why you can't be one of those few leaders. You don't have to be brighter than everyone else. There'll always be someone with more smarts than you, but it won't do him or her as much good if you excel in your ability to communicate.

34

Stress and Intensity Levels

Many new managers believe they should be able to arrange their work lives so that there will be no stress. But stress cannot be avoided. Occasionally, it will come calling. How you react to it is the key. You cannot always control what happens; what you can control is how you react to what happens to you.

Here's an interesting factor about stress that may make you feel better about the stress you feel early in your managerial career: Much of what seems stressful when you're new in management will seem ordinary and even mundane after you're experienced. This possibility reinforces the point that it may be your reaction and inexperience that causes you to consider it stress, rather than the situation itself. That may be a fine point, but the distinction seems significant.

Go back in your memory to the days you were taking driver education to learn how to safely operate an automobile. The first time you got behind the wheel was quite stressful. With experience, your ability to drive improved to the point that driving now seems as natural as brushing your teeth. The situation has not changed, but your experience and reaction to it has changed.

How you react to apparent stressful situations is part of your management style. Too many managers look so deep in thought. The brow is furrowed all the time. This demeanor is contagious to everyone working with you; unfortunately, it's contagious in a most negative way. However, a manager who can smile and be pleasant in what seems to be a stressful situation instills confidence in all who are working on the project.

It's hard to think clearly when you are uptight and nervous, so that reaction exacerbates the situation. That's a double whammy. You have a stressful situation, and your reaction diminishes your ability to bring it to a successful resolution.

The third whammy is the knowledge that says, "I'm going to be judged by how I handle this type of situation." That element adds even more pressure. Telling yourself not to get uptight is like someone telling you not to worry. It's much easier said than done.

There are those who believe that stressful situations get the juices flowing and bring out the best in people. You've heard the old saw, "When the going gets tough, the tough get going." I think that's true once you get over the fear of a stressful situation. Fear is like pouring the juices of stress down through a very small funnel.

React to the Problem, Not the Stress

To succeed, you must convert the fear of a stressful situation into the challenge of a stressful situation. If you are going to be a manager who periodically faces stressful situations, here are five suggestions that have worked for me:

1. Don't be panicked into impulsive action. It may make matters worse.
2. Take several deep breaths and try to relax. Speak slowly, even if you don't feel like it. This instills calm in those around you. It says, "He's not losing his head, and therefore I shouldn't."
3. Reduce the situations to two or three key points that could be handled to remove the urgency of the moment, so that the rest of it can be processed in a nonurgent way.
4. Assign three or four major elements to members of the

staff to process in parts and then be combined into the whole.
5. Ask for suggestions and ideas from the experienced members of your staff.

Not knowing the kind of business you are in, I cannot be more specific than that. But this kind of thought process alone (even if it's not 100 percent appropriate) gets you thinking straight. You're now thinking about the problem and not your reaction to it.

View yourself as an actor playing the role of the wise, calm, and decisive leader. Play that role to the hilt, and after a while it will cease being role-playing and will be you. This constitutes changing your reaction to the stressful situation.

Have Confidence in Your Abilities

As a manager, you handle tougher questions than those that came to you before the promotion. If they were all easy, anyone could solve them. You are there because someone saw in you the ability to deal with these more difficult situations. As you move up the corporate ladder, the problems become more complex, or so it seems. The important thing to remember is that your experience will remove most of the stress. When you've been a manager for a while, you will not react the same way, to the same situation, as you did the first few months in your managerial career. *It will get better.*

In the early days in management, just having the job brings elements of stress. That's why so many new managers look intense, as though they are carrying the weight of the world. While the concern and the desire to perform well is commendable, the intensity gets in the way of getting the job done. You are managing people in the tasks they need to complete in order to achieve a desired result. You are not leading them out of the trenches, with bayonets at the ready, across a minefield to engage the enemy in hand-to-hand combat.

I once had a seminar attendee ask me this question at the

afternoon break: "When we conclude today, would you give me a shorthand phrase that I can use for my management style?" This came from a very intense young woman.

The two words were "Lighten up."

35

The Complete Person

The first-time manager becomes engrossed in the new responsibilities and the job occupies almost every waking moment. This dedication is admirable, because it indicates that the person is determined to do a great job and be successful as a member of the management team.

But life must have a balance. While your career is important, it is not your entire life. Actually, you will be a more complete manager if you are a more complete person. You cannot separate the two.

I conducted a seminar at a college on the subject of preparing for retirement. It was designed for people who were within two years or less from retirement. At the beginning of the session, I went around the room and asked everybody to give his or her name and the number of years to go to retirement. We ended with a man who gave his name and said "I'm already retired."

I asked, "Well, how do you like retirement so far?" He didn't answer, but started crying aloud. He was embarrassed, and so I did not pursue it in front of the other attendees. However, I did have several conversations with him on the breaks. This man had lost his sense of identity and sense of worth. The job was his life, and when he retired he lost his identity. He was not a complete person. His interests, other than his family, all revolved around his career.

When you ask people what they do, they will automatically tell you what they do for a living. They are a dentist, or accountant, lawyer, salesperson, manager, barber, or trucker.

But we all do and are so much more than what we do to earn our daily bread—or if we're not, we should be.

A person whose only interest is the job is a one-dimensional individual, and a one-dimensional person is not as effective a manager as a multidimensional person.

I'm not referring to your first few months on the job. But after you have successfully passed through the breaking-in period, you need to broaden your interests and your activities.

Community Work

Everyone who aspires to management needs to be involved in the community. You don't take from a community and not put something of yourself back into it. The same is true of your profession. Put something back into your professional associations. These are not completely altruistic recommendations. The primary objective is to be of assistance to the cause of the profession, but there are ancillary benefits. You become known within your community and your profession. You enhance your base of knowledge, and you make some nice contacts and friends. That not only makes you a broader-based manager but also a more promotable one. And the higher you go in the organization, the more important leadership becomes. Community and professional association leadership is viewed most favorably in the executive suite of an overwhelming number of companies.

I have known of several situations where two people being considered for promotion were both qualified as far as the work was concerned. It was a close call, and the difference came down to leadership within and *outside* the halls of the company.

Outside Reading

While it is vital that you read about your business, it is also important that the manager be a well-read person. A manager should be a well-informed citizen and should know what's going on in her city, state, and nation. That means keeping up-to-date by reading newspapers, news magazines, and the trade magazines of your industry. A manager needs to be well informed about the world. What's going on in the world does affect your organization.

It also helps to read a good novel once in a while. Good fiction writers often have great insight into the human condition. Besides, these books are entertaining, and that's positive too.

All people at all stages of their lives need to stay mentally challenged and alert. It's much easier to do that if you maintain broad-based interests.

Conclusion

I've covered a variety of topics in this book on how to lead people, but certainly not every situation you'll confront in your career as a manager—or even within the first few weeks in your new role.

There's no way that a book of this sort can be made all-inclusive. I can only hope that I've given you some insight into the techniques of managing people that will make the job more meaningful and understandable. You may think that I've spent an inordinate amount of time on attitudes, on how you view yourself and the problems you face, but that's exactly where your success or failure in working with people will be determined—in your head.

If you're the type of person who believes you're primarily controlled by events, then what's the use? You're then merely a puppet with some giant puppet master pulling the strings. But in actuality it's not that way. Although events beyond your control do have an impact on your life, you control how and what you think. That in turn controls your reaction to these events.

I haven't conned you in this book. I haven't told you that if you work hard and keep your nose clean you'll rise to the top. However, I do think you'll have a better chance if you follow some of these concepts than if you ignore what to me are basic truths. You didn't come into this world with any guarantee that everything would be fair and that the deserving would always get what they deserve. They don't! However, you obviously have no chance to achieve your goals if you just sit there and wait for lightning to strike.

We must grow. This book is devoted to exploring how you manage your people, but I'm just as interested in seeing you grow as a total person. I believe your career can add to your total growth, since it's such a large part of your life. We shouldn't work at a job we don't like, but on the other hand we must be realistic in recognizing that all careers contain aspects we don't like. It's the balance that's important. If most of the job is enjoyable, ego-satisfying, and challenging, then you can put up with the few parts you don't care for. If it's the other way around and you dislike most of what you have to do, you're obviously in the wrong career and you ought to change it. Life is too short to spend time and energy in a career that destroys you.

I have known people, and perhaps you have too, who'll stick with a job they don't like because someday it will provide a great retirement benefit. What good does that prospective retirement benefit do if people ruin their health before they get to retirement? What's worse, they might not live that long.

There are also people around who will complain about a job constantly but will never seek a better job because their fear of change or the unknown is more powerful than their dislike of the job. Some people prefer the predictable (even if it's bad) over something new or unknown.

Perhaps Abraham Lincoln was right when he said, "Most people are about as happy as they make up their minds to be." That summarizes what I've tried to say throughout this book about the primacy of attitudes.

Too many people, as they approach their middle years, start thinking in terms of the kind of contribution they're making to the world. They often become depressed because they believe what they're doing is not very important. They ask themselves, "How significant is it that I'm a manager in a company making bolts?" Put in that context, it may not seem terribly relevant. But the question that should be asked is, "What kind of impact am I having on the people I come in contact with, both in my work and in my personal life?"

If you can answer that question in a positive way, then it

doesn't matter if the company you're associated with is making bolts or life-saving medicine. The system isn't the payoff; the product isn't the payoff; your impact on the people whose lives you touch is what's important. Also, holding a position that's a little higher on the organization chart *does not* make you more important than they are. An executive or a manager is a combination of leader and servant. Not many executives are willing to accept the servant aspect of their responsibilities, because it interferes with their exalted opinion of their rank.

In developing systems for your people to use, you're in fact serving them. In maintaining a salary administration and performance appraisal system, you're serving them. In working out vacation schedules that will allow your people to maximize the benefits of their relaxation time, you're serving them. In hiring and training quality people for your department, you're serving the people who are already there.

Most people have no difficulty understanding the proposition that the President of the United States has immense power but is also a servant—in fact, the number one public servant. The same concept applies to managerial jobs. There's a combination of what appear to be contradictory concepts: authority and a responsibility to serve. If you can keep these in some semblance of balance, I think you'll avoid getting an inflated view of your own importance. You'll also do a better job.

You don't necessarily get smarter. You gain more experience, which many people mistake for wisdom. It doesn't matter what you call it as long as you continually become more effective. You become more effective as you develop a greater variety of experiences in working with people. You gain little from repeating the same experiences except a smoothness that might not otherwise develop.

And the point, although elementary, bears repetition: There's a great deal to be gained from developing empathy for your subordinates' attitudes and feelings. Can you really sense how you'd want to be treated if you were in their position?

I truly wish the best for you as you direct people in what amounts to nearly one-half of their waking hours. Your success as a manager starts with you and your attitude toward that responsibility. If this book has been of some help to you, then its author is deeply gratified.

Index

action, vs. attitude, 154
advance notice of meetings, 186–187
age, managers vs. subordinates, 135–137
agenda, availability before meeting, 186
alcohol, 55–56
appreciation, 49–50
appropriateness, and humor, 184
arrogance, 152
attitude, 204
   about mistakes, 152–153
   determining in job interview, 76, 77–79
   of new employees, 75
   toward training, 85–86
   vs. action, 154
attitude talk, with new employee, 84–85
authority, 11–12, 149
autocrat, 44–45, 131, 148
avoidance—avoidance conflict, 82

balance
   details vs. general, 31–32
   in life style, 201–203
boss
   dealings with, 36–40
   job applicant's description of previous, 78, 79
   point of view of, 188
   unreasonable, 38–39
breadth of know-how, 30
buy-outs, firing employees after, 95

career development, 164
chairing committees, 189–190
change, 29–32
   detailed to general, 30
   in employees, 51–59
   manager's view of, 29
   managing, 59–60

   in operation methods, 10
   resistance to, 82
   upward or outward, 30
class, 191–192
cleanliness, 69
"closed-office" procedure, 170
coffee breaks, 14
comfort zone, 13, 52
   operational changes and, 58
comfort-zone underachiever, 81–82
committees
   advantages of, 189
   chairing, 189–190
communication
   at multiple levels, 33
   and career development, 164
   conversation terminators, 23–24
   grapevine, 181–182
   public speaking, 193–196
   with subordinates, 10
   written, 172–175
community work, 202
comprehension gap, 21
confidence, 198
   building, 16–19
   quiet, 155–156
   in stressful situations, 199–200
   in subordinates, 5
consistency, 98
conversation terminators, 23–24
coworkers, new manager tested by, 9
credit, 192
cross-training, 62

daydreaming, 171
decision making, 18–19, 37–38
   confidence in, 155–156
   subordinate input into, 17